AF341985

Rhetorical Readings, Dark Comedies, and Shakespeare's Problem Plays

UNIVERSITY PRESS OF FLORIDA

Florida A&M University, Tallahassee
Florida Atlantic University, Boca Raton
Florida Gulf Coast University, Ft. Myers
Florida International University, Miami
Florida State University, Tallahassee
University of Central Florida, Orlando
University of Florida, Gainesville
University of North Florida, Jacksonville
University of South Florida, Tampa
University of West Florida, Pensacola

Rhetorical Readings, Dark Comedies, and Shakespeare's Problem Plays

IRA CLARK

University Press of Florida
Gainesville · Tallahassee · Tampa · Boca Raton
Pensacola · Orlando · Miami · Jacksonville · Ft. Myers

12 11 10 09 08 07 6 5 4 3 2 1

Library of Congress Cataloging-in-Publication Data:
Clark, Ira.
Rhetorical readings, dark comedies, and Shakespeare's problem plays / Ira Clark.
p. cm.
Includes bibliographical references and index.
ISBN-13: 978-0-8130-3040-1 (alk. paper)
1. Shakespeare, William, 1564–1616—Tragicomedies.
2. English language—Early modern, 1500–1700—Rhetoric. 3. Shakespeare, William, 1564–1616. Measure for measure. 4. Shakespeare, William, 1564–1616. All's well that ends well. 5. Shakespeare, William, 1564–1616. Troilus and Cressida. 6. Shakespeare, William, 1564–1616—Literary style. 7. Shakespeare, William, 1564–1616—Language. I. Title.
PR2981.5.C57 2007
823.2'29–dc22 2006023150

The University Press of Florida is the scholarly publishing agency for the State University System of Florida, comprising Florida A&M University, Florida Atlantic University, Florida Gulf Coast University, Florida International University, Florida State University, University of Central Florida, University of Florida, University of North Florida, University of South Florida, and University of West Florida.

University Press of Florida
15 Northwest 15th Street
Gainesville, FL 32611-2079
http://www.upf.com

Contents

Apologia and Acknowledgments

Writing *Professional Playwrights*, I became committed to understanding sociological approaches for considering drama—primarily because so many playwrights seemed to work from notions similar to those of social psychologists. Both set scenarios for characters/experimental subjects to play out, imagining and discovering how they would behave. That is, much that is valuable in sociological studies—from principles promulgated by symbolic interactionism, through microanalyses of daily life, to theoretical proposals by Pierre Bourdieu and especially Anthony Giddens—appears to work out for us the traditional world as theater trope that playwrights worked through during the greatest era of English drama, maybe of any drama anywhere anytime. In a series of essays some of which culminated in *Comedy, Youth, Manhood in Early Modern England*, I pursued this cluster of ideas, realizing that many of the best social analyses came by way of comedies, particularly dark comedies, or satiric comedies, or problem comedies that appeared as Elizabeth's reign was giving way to James's. The principle I accepted from this exploration is that comedy is notable for its capacity to present difficult, even intractable personal and sociopolitical problems in a way not available to tragedy—precisely because comedy inculcates a distance, a wit that allows us to grapple with problems instead of evading them or emoting over them.

This comedic capacity comes under special pressure during a period that features dark, or black, or deeply satiric comedies that converge with tragedy or tragicomedy. One notable characteristic of such plays is their extraordinary mangling of generic horizons of expectation, even for a dramatic period that reveled in generic mongrelization. For different plays that we can categorize as problem plays have been variously considered tragic because their subjects are noble and some of their characters end up marred or destroyed, or tragicomic because of their mix of caste and their approach to the brink of disaster before miraculous discoveries and recoveries. In the earlier *Professional Playwrights* and *The Moral Art of Philip Massinger*, I considered the dominance of tragicomedy in the later Jacobean and Caroline drama, with its melodramatic posing of clashes of ideals and dire personal and sociopolitical problems only to resolve them through miraculous curative charity and forgiveness that reintegrate characters and communities. But this is a later solution to the dramatic difficulties posed by problem plays.

Other family resemblances also help to characterize problem plays, among which Shakespeare's *Troilus and Cressida*, *Measure for Measure*, and *All's Well That Ends Well* figure prominently for me. There remains more than a fundamental residue of problematic themes, issues, subject matter in current discussions of the problem plays. Recurring situations and character types and plotting devices provide another means of characterization. My history of our considerations outlines several modes of characterization that imply what these problem plays represent. But the most consistent earmark of problem plays seems to be their distinctive tone. So I focus on it last and, I hope, most tellingly. Because the term "problem play" names our difficulties with characterizing what it is, rather than not identifying what it is since we readily recognize one when we read it, I lean toward the old label. So I primarily employ it despite its manifest inadequacies of origin and historical usage and consequent ill repute. But I am not so committed to it as to exclude other labels.

A set of further working assumptions amounts to something of an intellectual genealogy. The first and most obvious here is that, in part because I have taught more Tudor-Stuart than Shakespeare drama during my career, I have long adhered to the opinion that too many Shakespeareans so focus on his work that they sacrifice insights available through the literary context and history of his dramatic peers. Such critics end up treating as if unique and individual what was interactive. A cluster of dramatists and companies in competition for audiences and livelihoods worked within the same traditions and mutually influenced each other. They borrowed and contributed, modified, reformed, and extended as they explored popular dramatic fads in styles, techniques, motivs. Specifically, then, I concluded that a useful approach to Shakespeare's problem plays or satiric plays or dark comedic plays was embedding consideration of them within the literary milieu of the most dominant popular form being written then, the set of plays identified for our time by Alfred Harbage and further recharacterized by his successors, his revisers.

A second working assumption is that every literary approach necessarily predetermines not the specific conclusion but the specific kind of conclusion to which it must lead. My critical predilections have oscillated between an old-fashioned literary and intellectual history I first learned as an undergraduate with N. T. Reid and Simon F. Kropp at New Mexico State, then developed as a graduate student with Z. S. Fink, Samuel Schoenbaum, and Phillip Harth at Northwestern, and a far different Leo Spitzer–inflected *explication de texte* sophisticated by Don Cameron Allen, Earl R. Wasserman, and Jackson I. Cope, to which I welded some reader-response techniques of Stanley E. Fish during my apprenticeship at Johns Hopkins. My studies have been generated now by the one impulse, then by the other. The problem with my earlier, historical impulse is its tedium and seeming irrelevance. Even if new historicism and cultural studies had taught us nothing more, still they would have made an invaluable contribution for compelling our attentive recognition that we inescapably create history that is primarily relevant to ourselves. The problem with my later, formal impulse is its inhumanity and deluded implication of objectivity. So the advantage I see in a broadly construed rhetorical approach is that it can mediate between the two impulses and thereby ameliorate the characteristic difficulties of each. Rhetoric works specifically with formal properties that set patterns and bounds for interpretations. Simultaneously rhetoric tests their potential effects on audiences within historical contexts. Moreover, it remains adaptable because it keeps at the fore its awareness that any formal technique or set of techniques can lead, depending on situating conditions, to a multitude of contrary audience effects. Thus it has the advantage of proffering a test of the adequacy of various historical explanations, of providing a mode of accommodating them, and of supplying a means of generating ever more of them.

A third working assumption is that our sense of history is inevitably and inextricably entangled with our sense of our own time. Akin to but differing from other new formalists who foreground their history and embed in it their formal analyses, I foreground the formal analyses and embed in them my history. Moreover, while my rehearsal of the historical contours of rhetoric for Shakespeare and his fellows seems predictable, other elements of my history initially appear to be counterintuitive: first comes a history of responses made by historical and thematic critics who make their own characterizations and historical explanations of the "problem play" from a wide array of theoretical and ideological stances; next come historical summaries of critical contextualizations, explanations, and thematizations of Shakespeare's plays. I cheerfully and gratefully borrow and reformulate others' histories. The crucial point is that never could I have arrived here by merely cataloging formal features; always I had to attend to contexts, historical explanations from a multitude of proposed critical stances. In fact, though I could not have kept myself from heeding historical explanations, I made a self-conscious effort to heed them.

Thus my method resembles very much the rediscovery of readings by famously influential critics who worked intensive analyses of specific textual details into expansive interpretations, from Ernst Curtius and Erich Auerbach through Madeline Doran and Joel Fineman. Besides their generally linguistic and my more specifically rhetorical approach, my difference from one of their tendencies, I believe, follows from a fourth and a fifth working assumption. I affirm that multiple responses issue from the same formal features—the question is not one of any certain ideological and formal correspondence. Nor do I believe that every work has a particular dominant figure— some do and open up to my kind of investigation; some don't. Finally, I have no faith in any master figuration that enables us to understand our psychology or our rationality or our discourse.

Besides thanks to my teachers for historical and formal stimuli and for the fundamental principles that ground this study, I owe thanks to others for helping me till it. Colleagues Jim Paxson and Al Shoaf have given me specific advice on individual essays and on the manuscript as a whole—beyond influencing me through our students, our conversations, and our understandings of literature and literary study. Then readers and editors of *Style* helped in the formulation of the essays on chiasmus in Shakespeare and on the aphoristic and other trappings of *All's Well That Ends Well*, which appeared there in earlier forms. The editors have also generously granted permission to reprint augmented and revised versions of these essays, which appeared as "'Measure for Measure': Chiasmus, Justice, and Mercy," *Style* 35 (Winter 2001): 659–80, and as "The Trappings of *All's Well That Ends Well*," *Style* 39 (Fall 2005): 277–98 . Finally, two anonymous readers for the University Press of Florida and the Press's editors compelled me to face theoretical and disciplinary issues I had half-consciously evaded, to improve argumentative focus on theoretical and methodological relationships I had more intuited and implied than rationalized, to offer more overarching explanations in the beginning and more cohesive connections throughout, and to make my writing more readable. None of these donors, of course, bears any burden for my inadequacies in making this into the study they envisioned it might become.

1

Dark Comedies, Rhetoric, Shakespeare's Problem Plays

This collection of interrelated essays deals with the most popular, and the most troubling, kind of play written between the late 1590s, when the Elizabethan period was dying, and the early 1600s, when the Jacobean years were being born. They reconsider what are often called the problem plays or problem comedies or dark comedies that Shakespeare wrote about 1602 to 1605. My first essay sets a historical critical context for the formal ones to come. Each subsequent essay employs what could be called a formal rhetorical or quasi-rhetorical approach to one play. Since I begin with the smallest and move to the largest rhetorical focus I look at *Measure for Measure, All's Well That Ends Well,* and *Troilus and Cressida* in what is likely reverse chronological order.

Initially I am concerned with placing these plays so difficult to consider within what I take to be their primary historical literary context. They join in sharing, emulating, extending the troubling genre that calls to mind the comedies of John Marston, Thomas Middleton, and Ben Jonson, notable associations with comedies by George Chapman, Thomas Dekker, and John Webster, and a set of intermittently read comedies by the likes of Lording Barry, George Cooke, William Houghton, and Edward Sharpham. Interest in such a context has increased of late.[1] One suggestion likely to prove influential has been made by Jean E. Howard at the climax of her call for a set of revisions to generic classifications in *A Companion to Shakespeare*. "Shakespeare and Genre" proposes to study Shakespeare's plays with those around them; and it takes its impetus from theories of materialist formulations of self, particularly the relationships between gender, society, and governance. Howard's model examines the personal and sexual disorder in prostitution and whorehouses versus attempts at their control by magistrates through courts and prisons and by interventions of powerful princes across a number of plays. She particularly compares and contrasts both parts of Dekker's *The Honest Whore* to *Measure for Measure*. Another impressive recent account is Paul Yachnin's for *A Companion to Shakespeare's Works*. "Shakespeare's Problem Plays and the Drama of His Time: *Troilus and Cressida*, *All's Well That Ends Well*, *Measure for Measure*" applies to the plays a different materialist perspective, economics, in an approach he has christened "populuxe drama." He considers Shakespeare's radically inventive exploitation of traditions so as to capture a market in the theatrical competition for audience profits. And he specifically scrutinizes in the context of problem plays the strategies of "*Troilus*'s language and genre, *All's Well's* techniques of inward characterization, and *Measure*'s complex political perspective" (53). My more formal rhetorical and dramatic focus concentrates on figuration, aphorisms, diction, imagery, and other techniques that embed larger questions of style, structure, theme, and mode. So it could be seen to complement both Howard's consideration of sexual practices, social relations, and their civic control among a set of plays that include Shakespeare's and also Yachnin's examination of the same set of plays as strategies to woo paying audiences. It begins at a contrasting pole to the material. Yet it can end by contributing to our understanding of materialist issues by offering tests of current interpretations and stimulus for new ones.

By focusing on some dominant recurring rhetorical technique or cluster of them in each of Shakespeare's three problem plays, I hope to avoid difficulties roused by prevailing thematic studies. The primary potential difficulty is the predisposition to preferred sociopolitical and ideological results by the thematic focus and, closely following, the predetermination of confirming conclusions by the method of approach. It seems to me that such potential difficulties can be hedged against by considering the plays from the confessedly partial perspective of rhetorical forms. I have long been predisposed to the notion that formal analysis can describe recurring patterns in literature that enable thematic, allegorizing readings. For forms produce the coherence and cohesion, pattern and recurrence, that make possible logical or systematic explanations from the valuable perspectives of a multitude of disciplines and sociopolitical stances. In pursuit of the potential contribution to the study of literature and culture that understanding the forms of figures and stylistic traits might make, I take comfort in a recent resurgence of rather formal analyses of literature that make use of the many gains of historicist projects of the last quarter century.[2] I differ somewhat from most of these by my tendency to embed history within the forms whereas most tend to embed the formal discussions within their histories.

I take particular comfort in the increased heed to rhetorical approaches, broadly defined, from the last third of the twentieth century into the opening years of the twenty-first. "Shakespeare wrote in a culture almost as rhetorical as our own," Peter G. Platt introduces "Shakespeare and Rhetorical Culture."[3] In *Elizabethan Rhetoric: Theory and Practice*, Peter Mack has made a compelling case, if anyone harbored lingering doubts after Wayne A. Rebhorn's *The Emperor of Men's Minds*, for the informing power of rhetoric during the early modern era in England. Mack's comprehensive study makes a full case for the pervasive knowledge and use of rhetoric in early modern England through an examination of the specifics of rhetorical training in English grammar schools and universities along with the employment of its strategies, tactics, and techniques. He discusses the European manuals of rhetoric and native adaptations of them, and he analyzes the employment of the rhetorical skills inculcated, extending from quotidian entries in notebooks and familiar letters through more formal writing in histories, conduct manuals, and romances, to self-conscious arguments in political documents, parliamentary oratory, religious polemics, and sermons. There can be no doubt that rhetorical training and handbooks in early modern England produced practices in writing and reading.

Thomas Wilson, who stakes a strong claim for producing the earliest widely influential comprehensive English rhetoric, emphasizes an ethical appeal that follows a line of tradition from Aristotle. Thus his preface to *The Arte of Rhetorique* (1553) emphasizes the orator and his pragmatic base in fundamental beliefs, Wilson's own being founded in Christianized classicism. God granted Adam the personal appeal he promptly lost; then God restored the capability to Adam's offspring so as to civilize humanity. Thereby humans are renewed as the dominant animal because the reasonable one; we become virtual demigods on earth. Wilson's opening book focuses on the orator's relationship to his audience, teaching, delighting, and persuading them. So he follows as well the rhetorical line of Cicero's *De Oratore* and the pseudo-Ciceronian *Rhetorica ad Herennium* in its emphasis and measure of achievement in audience affect gained through ethos. In the first division of rhetoric, invention, come the topics central to the discovery of arguments for epideictic or panegyric oratory offering praise and blame, deliberative or legislative oratory for making decisions, and judicial oratory for making judgments. This is familiar from Aristotle and dominant from the focus on the formation of the perfect orator through the powerful influence of Cicero and Quintilian's *Institutio Oratoria*. Also with invention comes the significant emphasis on *in utramque partem*—seeking out arguments for both sides of a controversial issue—that Cicero adapted by following Isocrates' search for the persuasive since probable based on Carneades's philosophy of uncertainty. In the early modern era, rhetoricians generally extended the technique into an attitude open to ambivalence.[4] Influenced as well by Melanchthon and Agricola by way of Erasmus, Wilson covers much of this terrain more comprehensively in his *The Rule of Reason, conteining the Arte of Logique* (1551) that constitutes the companion to *The Art of Rhetorique*. One other major contribution attributable to invention is emphasized by Mack. The employment of books of proverbs, maxims, and other striking sayings as commonplaces was widespread, as in such popular works as Erasmus's *Adagia*. Disposition, the second division of rhetoric, concerns especially the seven parts of the oration and other outlines for persuasive presentation; here most generally under discussions of the exordium appear the three traditional appeals to logos, pathos, and ethos. Similar outlines appear in the letter-writing manuals, dominantly the frequently reprinted editions of William Fulwood's *Enemie of Idleness* (1568) and of Angel Day's *The English Secretary* (1586).

The third division of rhetoric, elocution or ornamentation, has continued to be the best-known and most bewritten since the *Rhetorica ad Herennium* and Quintilian's *Institutio Oratoria*—particularly during the Renaissance. This shift in attention, influenced by Ramus and Talon's severance of logic from rhetoric, was promoted by the familiar books with long listings that define or characterize and exemplify schemes and tropes. These stretch from Richard Sherry's *A Treatise of Schemes and Tropes* (1550) through Henry Peacham's *Garden of Eloquence* (1577, 1593) and George Puttenham's *The Arte of English Poesie* (1589) to John Hoskins's *Directions for Speech and Style* (1599). Besides such standard texts, letter-writing manuals also supply marginal notations and appendices that emphasize figurative language. All, heavily dependent on previous treatments, were extraordinarily popular because of the early modern era's desire to gain the fullness, *copia*, plenitude deemed necessary for the establishment of a respected literary language and culture. While the last two divisions of rhetorical study, memory and delivery, do not lack importance, the first three, invention, disposition, and elocution, wield the most influence on the drama and therefore on my study.[5] Proving to be of particular interest is elocution, for analysis of one powerful figure of language prominent in *Measure for Measure*, for descriptions of enhancing figurations in *All's Well That Ends Well*, and for the examination of styles in *Troilus and Cressida*. Concern with the employment of aphorisms, part of invention, is of special interest for *All's Well That Ends Well*. And the fundamental appeals to audience through pathos, logos, and particularly ethos, generally found in introductions and with disposition, are crucial to the interpretation of *Troilus and Cressida*.

I would extend the range of Mack's cautiously confined study by taking advantage of the broad scope of characterizations of what rhetoric is and of recent studies from which he dissociates himself.[6] For in the second half of the twentieth century there has been a revival in the influence of rhetoric on thought and scholarly work. To name Kenneth Burke, Chaim Perlman, Stephen Toulmin, and Jürgen Habermas recalls a renewed impetus, with greater depth and breadth of scholarship in rhetorical theory and practice and in their exchange of influence with other disciplines. The Renaissance can be considered a rhetorical culture that emphasized the third part of the trivium as the successor to a medieval grammatical and logical culture that emphasized the other two; now rhetoricians like to refer to the rhetorical turn of late twentieth-century thought as the successor to an earlier linguistic and logical culture.[7] A cursory review reveals that Walter Jost and Wendy Olmsted's *A Companion to Rhetoric and Rhetorical Criticism* deploys an extraordinary array of theoretical and practical scholars under the banner of rhetoric. The essays include theoretical and applied studies that range in history and genre from the beginnings of Western discourse to the present. Their focus extends from foundational assessments of audience and influence on deliberative, judicial, and panegyric occasions, across the employment of ethical, pathetic, and logical appeals, into the invention of political, scientific, and hermeneutic communities. They analyze the disposition of arguments in individual texts. And they consider the elocutionary in affective stylistics and poetics. The recent *Encyclopedia of Rhetoric* edited by Thomas O. Sloane opens up yet more new terrain for rhetoric, in forays carried out in traditional entries as well as in entries unanticipated twenty years ago. Consideration of memory as the ground of knowledge and of delivery's kinship to self-creation (or at least self-representation) by way of Stephen Greenblatt and its relationship to Judith Butler's performance theory is reviewed by Platt. To fail to take advantage of these developments would exclude valuable techniques for analysis and hide from our own history.

Richard A. Lanham and Brian Vickers have proved particular champions of rhetorical approaches among forerunners in recent Renaissance criticism.[8] Since then many helpful studies have appeared. A number have specifically influenced this one. Patricia Parker's new linguistic and rhetorical approach, inspired by deconstruction and informed by gender theory, new historicism, and cultural studies, has remained crucial for every essay. Jeanne Fahnestock's analysis of rhetorical figuration in science and Keir Elam's analysis of language games in Shakespeare's comedies are central to my study of chiasmus and *Measure for Measure*. Gerard Genette, Gary Saul Morson, and Phyllis Gorfain have proved general and specific inspirations for rhetorical extensions of wide employment of maxim and aphorism into riddle and challenge in narrative structure as well as in discourse through *All's Well That Ends Well*. Elizabeth Freund's deconstructionist examination of the play of language and reference in *Troilus and Cressida* provides major impetus, while Dilip Parmeshwar Gaonkar's analysis of the contingent probabilities of persuasion and Kenneth Burke's renewal of emphasis on the ethical appeal rest behind analyses of that play.

My dual interest in exemplifying the early modern employment and response to rhetoric simultaneously with contemporary tools of rhetorical analysis appears in several guises throughout this study. It is especially evident in my perhaps puzzling shift from this introduction to the first chapter. In this contextual section, I trace our critical preoccupation, since Alfred Harbage's grounding studies, with the troubling problem plays that dominated the late Elizabethan–early Jacobean stage. And I follow Harbage in allowing Shakespearean criticism to occupy an integral role in the history instead of giving it its customary separate story. From inception each version has referred to the other, but more often than not literary critics so focus either on Shakespeare or on Marston, Jonson, Middleton, and company that they imply what I take to be general developments are individual characteristics. Therefore, in order to understand the context as a whole, I characterize contributions made by studies of the multiple heritages, the genre, the mode, the style, and the sociopolitical issues bound up in problem plays. This label I employ despite its current disfavor in order to indicate the difficulties and the potential of the genre. For the critical context tracks a trajectory that indicates why these plays have gathered so much interest since the Second World War. In brief, for others throughout this period, as for Harbage, the problem plays have continued to proffer a highly charged approach to understanding some of our problems with national identity. But along the way our sense of what constitutes both these problem plays and that nationhood has been radically transformed. There has been an extraordinary focus on what Harbage left at the peripheries of the problem plays, based on different ideological stances from his and from multiple disciplines. The result is a new focus on the city and on its interactions in a host of realms that declares a sense of the incipient nationhood and national identity opposed to that Harbage described. But the new focus reviews the very ground Harbage surveyed. Thus he remains invaluable to our opposed understanding.

Next in this chapter, in order to establish a basis for further study of the rhetoric of Shakespeare's problem plays I characterize a general stylistics of problem plays exemplified by the well-known *The Malcontent*, *The Alchemist*, *A Chaste Maid in Cheapside*, *The Widow's Tears*, and the less familiar *The Fleer*. This style is comprised of first, a diction marked by neologisms and polysyllables in collision with a talk vulgar, sexual, scatological, and full of puns; second, an exalted rhetoric of repetitions, parallels, balances, and schemes most often versified in competition with a base, generally prosaic, irregular, and disruptive syntax; third, a high density of virtuosic figuration that is involved, mixed, and often obscure; fourth, a frequency of brief satiric characterizations; and fifth, a high incidence of sententious, analytic, and self-serving proverbs. While all of these characterizations prove useful to consideration of all the plays, the first two and the fourth specifically indicate a useful approach to the styles of *Troilus and Cressida*. The third provides entry to the dominant complex and showy figure of *Measure for Measure*. And the last together with the third lead to the specific and the global patterns of *All's Well That Ends Well*.

In the essays interpreting individual plays I take advantage of rhetoric's expansive disciplinary bounds to follow out rhetorical considerations. I open with a straightforward analysis of a prevalent rhetorical scheme, the kind taught, deployed, and admired widely in early modern England and featured in the ostentatious figuration of problem plays. Chiasmus can be used for clever self-display and clowning, but even more it can be used to emphatically compare and contrast alternatives and to focus and compel choices about preference, equivalence, value, and justice. During this characterization I examine many complex uses of chiasmus throughout Shakespeare's works. Next I offer a brief example of its use to reinforce dominant political norms in *2 Henry IV*. Finally I extend its pervasive use in presenting arrays of vexing and perplexing moral and theological, social and political issues in *Measure for Measure* so as to argue that this problem play, like many others, does not so much present any theme or set of themes as it presents a set of contentious and intractable issues as irresolvable. This further implies that *Measure for Measure*, like other problem plays, is deeply engaged in the difficult issues of that day.

I proceed to *All's Well That Ends Well* by way of broader consideration of aphoristic language that generally sums up wisdom in proverbs, stimulates consideration of understanding in aphorisms, and analyzes actors and actions. While blatant, the predominant use of such brief, memorable sayings in *All's Well That Ends Well* is not merely the witty self-display of rhetorical devices or trappings and jocular social interactions. Instead the characters primarily employ aphorisms with other stylistic techniques such as recurring image references to challenge and attack each other; then they repeatedly employ these to entrap each other. Thus they replicate one defining characteristic of problem comedies in the era: the display of wit as characters devise scheming intrigues to gain sexual, economic, and sociopolitical advantages in fierce competition. *All's Well* varies this pattern by making a young woman rather than a young gallant the victor in this social and sexual battle of wits. Moreover, Shakespeare replicates and varies the dominant patterns of intrigue plotting notable in problem comedies by offering a series of reversals that constitute false temporary conclusions to the play before presenting the extensive climactic set of surprising and revealing reversals that reaffirm his heroine's witty victory in the battle of the sexes and society.

I conclude the interpretive essays by returning to a more traditional sense of rhetoric as a mode of ethical appeal that employs displays of style to engage and influence audiences. I analyze *Troilus and Cressida* as showing three modes of wit that influence others more than as a general preoccupation with decadence and disgust. Here I consider three major stylistic clusters named after their three primary users, the persuasive directors and commentators who set the tone of the play. All three styles (statements of received opinion so as to promote shrewd analyses and plans based on these givens, the wit of Ulysses; interactive social contact, the wit of Pandarus; and scurrilous analytic commentary, the wit of Thersites) are dependent on appreciative estimates by the audiences to whom they are addressed. Most significantly, this appreciation is based on a principle of reflexivity, that is, the speaker's sense of how he is perceived by his audience, a principle that is reciprocal. Obviously true of the wit of Pandarus, the paradigm holds for the other styles as well. In fact, these styles are used persuasively by many speakers. The Trojan council offers an epitome of the three styles but especially of how despite a nigh flawless argument based on logos, pathos is more dominant still and ethos proves to be the decisive determinant. For the emotional appeal to the self-reflexive principle of masculine "honor" drives the outcome. By presenting such issues in such a self-conscious and self-indicting, not to say cynical, manner, *Troilus and Cressida*, as well as *Measure for Measure* and *All's Well That Ends Well*, declares its membership among the problem plays that dominated late Elizabethan and early Jacobean theater.

Finally, I make a brief plea for rhetorical and formal study as a useful entry to these plays, to others, and perhaps to other forms of discourse. And I consider how the analysis of forms in texts aids in understanding thematic studies, offering a gauge for evaluating interpretations, a mode of accommodating them, and a stimulus for proliferating them. Recent formal studies proffer opportunity to understand themes more distinctly and more fully by further exploiting the potential we have gained through the recent concentration on new historicism, the perspectives provided by the social sciences, particularly materialist ones, feminist and gender studies, and other advances.

2

Dominant English Comedy at the Turn of the Seventeenth Century

By writing *Shakespeare and the Rival Traditions* at the middle of the twentieth century, Alfred Harbage focused scholarly attention on the tone of forty-three "satirical comedies" out of fifty-five extant plays produced for the English stage between 1599 and 1613 (71).[1] This is not to say that Harbage initiated the interest. The label "problem plays" was introduced in *Shakespeare and His Predecessors* by Frederick S. Boas, who, trying to explain *Hamlet* as well as *Measure for Measure, All's Well That Ends Well, and Troilus and Cressida*, adapted it from the late nineteenth-century realism of Ibsen, Strindberg, and Shaw. In 1931 W. W. Lawrence had considered historical and folkloric backgrounds to address the difficult tone in *Shakespeare's Problem Comedies*, and in 1938 Oscar James Campbell had examined satiric settings created by Shakespeare, Jonson, Marston, Middleton, and others for *Comicall Satyre and Shakespeare's "Troilus and Cressida."* But the history of "problem plays," especially for Shakespeareans, continues to constitute a troubled usage for reluctant users. As outlined by Carol Thomas Neely, "problem plays" was usually employed early on to negotiate between a supposed crisis in Shakespeare's life and a critical antipathy to these few plays, a stance since abandoned. Later on "problem plays" has generally been employed to indicate the vexed subject matter and treatment of adolescent sexuality in this group of plays.[2] But in consideration of "problem plays" as a set Shakespeareans have unduly narrowed the range of multiple, complex, intertwined issues in society, politics, economics, religion, and other domains in history and criticism that have been emphasized by scholars of the individual Shakespeare plays and of related plays by Shakespeare's peers.[3] Moreover, generally critics studying these plays have bracketed off more formal generic, linguistic and stylistic, and rhetorical approaches. So, to return to the ground Harbage surveyed and that still remains beneath all our studies of problematic comedies of the last several years of the sixteenth century and the first decade of the seventeenth implicitly expands concerns again. This expansion specifically includes our own critical responses to an ill-defined set of plays as a means to more nearly understand two different times, then when they were first presented and now when we are construing them within a set of values alien to Harbage.

Harbage made two sustaining contributions. First, his account merged theatrical history with dramatic history in his explanation that different companies in different playhouses offered different repertoires to different audiences. Companies playing in "public theaters" for an audience of wide-ranging social and economic backgrounds offered a wholesome democratic spectacle to the populace. Companies playing in pricier "private theaters" for an audience of courtiers, inns of court members, and aspirants to such status offered jaundiced perspectives to an oversophisticated and cynical privileged coterie. Second, Harbage's fundamental premise was that in the contention between the two contrasting kinds, "public theater" was more valuable for the rising nation of England, the United Kingdom, the world dominated by a western European and U.S. American *translatio imperii* and *translatio studii*. The triumphant and uplifting Shakespearean ideals of a patriotic Christian humanism's promotion of a divine plan, the dignity of man, a chaste and faithful heterosexual monogamy, and the commonweal (tracking his chapters that characterize "Two Views of Life") has proved superior. The jaded, materialist questions posed by atheists and agnostics, jaundiced critics, libertines, and social and economic malcontents on the fringes of the dominant society have proved inferior. Of less importance for my unfair caricature of Harbage's influential vision of the theater of Shakespeare's era is how dated it now seems, how much a part of the value system for which World War II was fought and celebrated through the early years of the cold war. Of major importance is how much Harbage's rejected vision continues to focus our historical and critical attention, even after important political shifts and scholarly extensions, challenges, and revisions. To understand the now obscured influence of his contribution we need to look at some extensions, critiques, and hypotheses so as to gather some idea of the breadth, depth, and complexity of the debate and its potential for addressing a multitude of questions about the problem plays at the time of their inception and at the time of our interpretations. For these are the issues that will underlie the individual studies. Then, on this grounding, I can recall my proposal that one of the most useful approaches for addressing all contentions and perspectives is what can be broadly characterized as rhetoric extended because the other issues are embedded in its formal concerns.

Harbage's Ground: A Resurvey

The initial difficulty for any study of tone in the problem plays written when James was inheriting the throne is the rich quarry of traditions that scholars have discovered to be significant influencing them. Proposed theatrical determinants include the reemergence of children's companies and the subsequent "war of the theaters" over prospective supporting audiences, the "poetomachia" that pitted Thomas Dekker and John Marston against Ben Jonson inside the coterie theater, and Will Shakespeare's alleged intervention criticizing both sides and championing a more inclusive theater. Proposed tonal and ideological determinants include the popular interest in and employment of satire's techniques and functions, the influence of continental sophistication via Italianate revenge and intrigue narratives, and the impulse summed up in Machiavellism and Montaigne's skeptical meditations on French culture. Proposed generic determinants include the development of a satiric city comedy from native traditions that intermingled commercial and sexual interests alongside an existing promotional citizen comedy. And proposed situational determinants include the development of London into the site of nascent English nationhood these comedies helped define or at least through which we conceive it.

In *Children of the Revels* Michael Shapiro extended Harbage's studies back to the early modern beginnings of the boy companies, their venues, audiences, and styles of performance. So he provided for Harbage's conclusions a fuller context, a more sophisticated genealogy, and a larger array of dramatic genres. After the initial Henrician development of court entertainments and the subsequent innovative Elizabethan formalizations of design and style by John Lyly, the final phase of plays emerged with the reemergence of the children's companies as early as 1597, somewhat earlier than Harbage's 1599. Then "comical satire" and city comedy increased the proportion of denigrating laughter at those who lacked the social and intellectual status and cachet of aspirants to courtly circles—the gulls of useless pedantry, restrictive puritanism, grasping usury, and citizen commerce, and as well the gulls who lacked wit and *sprezzatura*. It thereby elevated an audience who assumed their own sophistication.

The central challenge to Harbage's antithetical Shakespearean audiences, and the crucial revision, came from the social history of theater. In *The Privileged Playgoers of Shakespeare's London* Ann Jennalie Cook refuted the demographic data of Harbage's earlier book and so demolished his national versus coterie, wholesome versus decadent "rival traditions" dependent on the contrast between audiences. Cook pointed out that the middle-class citizens who mainly peopled Harbage's national audience were an anachronistic projection onto middling and laboring folk who did not possess the resources to sustain Elizabethan stage companies at public theaters, much less private ones. Profitable repertory theater required the sustaining audience privileged by birth, achievements, or training, and especially leisure and wealth to regularly attend performances. In "Shakespeare's Unprivileged Playgoers, 1576–1642" Martin Butler overreacted, but exploited Cook's vulnerabilities of overstatement and severe constriction of the privileged audience. She had virtually excluded groups referred to in prologues and plays and described in contemporary accounts; in effect, she had restricted the audience to the one associated with coterie theaters.[4] In *Playgoing in Shakespeare's London* Andrew Gurr provides a more nuanced accommodation between the stereotypes proposed by Harbage and Cook. Gurr's characterization is based on three new estimates. One follows from the two types of theater, now less polemically labeled amphitheater (open to the sky and accommodating much larger audiences) and hall (covered, smaller, and much more expensive). A second describes a fuller range of possible members of audiences based on contemporary references. And a third considers the shifts in attendance throughout the period between the beginnings and the closing of professional theaters in London. In the 1990s Gurr produced *The Shakespearian Playing Companies*, which for some scholars promises still more sophisticated correspondences of playhouses and companies with audience tastes. Roslyn Lander Knutson's *Playing Companies and Commerce in Shakespeare's Time* narrows the potential by noting that both kinds of companies and theaters featured all kinds of plays but leaves unchallenged the description of the preponderance of satiric comedies (56, 63). Since many playwrights were writing for both amphitheaters and hall theaters, since many of the plays saw performances at both kinds of theaters by both kinds of companies, and since plays got traded among companies, the audiences and presumably their preferences and inclinations overlapped considerably. A large spectrum of positions was presented to them. Thus the current status of our knowledge of audiences and theaters suggests that judging the satiric tone of comedies popular at James's accession is no simple task of calculating the effects on audiences of certain theaters and companies but instead of reconsidering the complexities of the plays themselves.

The late nineteenth century discovered a hall theater "poetomachia" that pitted Thomas Dekker and John Marston against Ben Jonson. James P. Bednarz has revived and enhanced the hypothesis at the beginning of the twenty-first century to characterize and explain the change in comic tone at the Tudor-Stuart transition. In his reconstruction for *Shakespeare and the Poets' War*, Bednarz places Shakespeare center stage as the dominant writer of comedy against whose achievements Jonson began defining a new comedy of railing in *Everyman Out of His Humour* (1599).[5] Shakespeare was involved with his own company's production of *Everyman Out* at the Globe. Shakespeare knew the satiric caricatures of Jonson by Marston through *Histriomastix*, *Jack Drum's Entertainment*, and *What You Will* for the Children of Paul's at the chapel theater, and by Marston and Dekker in *Satiromastix* at both Paul's and the Globe; Shakespeare knew as well Jonson's countering caricatures of Marston and Dekker in *Everyman Out*, then *Cynthia's Revels* and *The Poetaster* for the Children of the Chapel at Blackfriars. Ultimately Shakespeare appropriated and incorporated this new satiric comedy within a kinder skeptical comedy. But immediately he used *Troilus and Cressida* so as to present caricatures of Marston and Jonson, purging the latter, and implicitly so as to critique railing comedy. Some such theory of competition among companies and playwrights can contribute to grounding our understanding of the "comical satire" that became dominant at the turn of the seventeenth century. And a less combative version can place Shakespeare among competitors seeking to attract and hold a paying audience.

When Harbage dedicated *Shakespeare and the Rival Traditions* to Oscar James Campbell he honored Campbell for the founding contribution summed up in *Comicall Satyre and Shakespeare's "Troilus and Cressida."* Campbell hypothesized that poets who had been intensely interested in verse satire for a decade adapted the mode for the stage in response to the bishops' edict on 1 June 1599, which ordered many satires destroyed and forbade their further publication. He drew to critical attention the traditions of classical verse satire as a ground for the popular new tone. Twenty years after Campbell's book, Alvin Kernan's *The Cankered Muse* consolidated and extended Campbell's literary history into a more theoretically based critical description of the genre, one that continues to frame our stylistic discussions of the satirical comedies (and tragedies) of the first decade of the seventeenth century. Kernan initiated his contribution by positing three foci of satire as a genre—the chaotic scene teeming with fools and knaves, the static plot, and the melancholy and indignant satirist persona. Then he centers on the Elizabethans' false but extraordinarily popular and useful etymology of satire issuing from the shaggy and rough, passionate and lusty, plainspoken and envious satyr of ancient satyr plays. The harsh Juvenalian tone of railing against the time's ubiquitous and overwhelming failures and immoralities, which dominated verse satires of the 1590s, was imported into satiric plays. The innovative poet and playwright was John Marston through the formal verse satires *Pigmalions Image and Certain Satyres* and *The Scourge of Villainy* and then later through the plays *What You Will* and *The Malcontent*. Marston and other combatants in the "poetomachia," preeminently Ben Jonson, demonstrated what the conversion could achieve. Eminent is the railing satyric vulgar style (in every sense) that perpetually undercuts an inflated hyperbole's exaltation of the physical and vicious.

A pair of imported, less definite yet vital determinants of the dark comic tone popular on stage at James's accession appears briefly yet tellingly in Harbage's considerations: the attractive yet repellant continental sophistication attributable to Italianate revenge and Machiavellian intrigue and to Montaigne's skepticism about French culture. The important study of Machiavellism in the new tone is G. K. Hunter's "English Folly and Italian Vice" from 1960, elaborated through his introductions to editions of John Marston's plays and culminating in his late 1990s "The Boy Actors and the New Dramaturgy" in *English Drama, 1586–1642*, his volume for the *Oxford History of English Literature*. Hunter takes for his text lines from the prologue to the second part of Marston's *Antonio and Mellida, Antonio's Revenge*. These dismiss anyone "Who winks and shuts his apprehension up / From common sense of what men were, and are, / Who would not know what men must be." Then Hunter demonstrates that Marston approaches Jonson's satire not from a comic but from a tragic heritage. Marston differs from his tragic forebears in that his satiric scene, not the tragic actor and action, becomes the focus; he differs from his comic counterpart in that his satire gets dispersed through the lines of different actors rather than emanating from one satiric persona. Marston transports a view of Italy from Machiavelli's and Guicciardini's histories almost a century old, an Italy analyzed realistically for manipulation more than eulogized for inspiring ideals. Later Marston consolidates the satiric and the Machiavellian, the viewpoint and the manipulator, in the deposed Altofront disguised as the satirist Malevole in *The Malcontent*. These patterns get disseminated through other satiric comedies with disguised satirist manipulators. One line leads from Marston's own duke Hercules as the Fawn in *Parasitaster, or The Fawn*, and Freevill as the pimp Don Dubon in *The Dutch Courtesan*, through Edward Sharpham's banished Duke of Florence Antifront as the serving man Fleer to his courtesan daughters in *The Fleer*. A prominent exemplar is Thomas Dekker and John Webster's Justiniano, the Italian merchant obsessed with his wife's fidelity as the writing master Parenthesis in *Westward Ho*. While there has been no overarching study of Montaigne's influence on the dark comedies of the early 1600s, Philip J. Finkelpearl's *John Marston of the Middle Temple* provides an influential study of Montaigne's importance for Marston's *The Dutch Courtesan* (198ff). Finkelpearl describes Marston's reliance for stance and inspiration on Montaigne's arguments that prostitution makes a natural, understandable masculinist response to the inevitable physical lusts that cannot be constrained by unreasonable and unbending, ultimately destructive codes of conduct. Consequently prostitution provides a socially useful if morally tainted outlet that safeguards marriage and lineage.

Both Machiavelli's and Montaigne's impact on the history of ideas or ideologies by way of their challenges to Christianity and humanism helped shape the questions and attitudes presented in the dark comedies around 1600. Since the mid-twentieth century, Machiavelli's realpolitik and Montaigne's skepticism could be viewed as central to Hiram Haydn's exposition of *The Counter-Renaissance*, a work that regularly turns to the problem plays for evidence. Montaigne plays a central role in questioning the confidence in reason's capacity to understand if there is any teleology, any ordained ordering of the world. Montaigne and Machiavelli both play major roles in the skeptical undermining of rationalist universal laws. Montaigne insists on a sense of relative truths as beliefs based on various cultural traditions rather than truth as God-given. Machiavelli recognizes the human origins and maintenance of civil law in self-defense and self-promotion based on what amounts to force and fraud on behalf of the state; and he maintains that claims of law's divine origin are invoked only as a justification. Both thinkers base their assertions on a realist or naturalist challenge to the prevalent alternatives of either spiritualizing or devaluing the physical. Both ultimately posit mankind's fundamental membership in the animal world, Montaigne seeking the morality of temperance in order to attain pleasure and Machiavelli advocating political efficacy in a *virtù* that makes the most of *fortuna*'s vicissitudes. Toward the end of the century Haydn's Machiavelli and Montaigne gathered inflections of Marxian, Foucauldian, and Brechtian concerns with materialism and power relations through Jonathan Dollimore's *Radical Tragedy*.[6] Dollimore also supplied nuanced descriptions of inconsistencies internal to any belief system due to clashing residual, dominant, and emergent motivs. Haydn's "decentralizing" and "individualizing" become Dollimore's "demystifying," "dislocating" of Christian providence, and "decentering" of humanist essentialism. For Dollimore Machiavelli unmasks the fraud of invoking religion to justify the use of power in politics; he is succeeded by Hobbes. And Montaigne provides the skeptical realism that discovers the cultural relativism of laws; his "custom" is rediscovered in Althusser's "ideology." Both influences contribute to a new sense of political and social materialism or realism in Jacobean drama, a movement identified by Brecht with epic theater that challenges providentialism and essentialism.

A crucial however indefinite native English contribution to the problem plays was examined by literary historians and critics who were looking less to characterize what Harbage heard in them than to describe a genre of satiric city comedy preoccupied with London's environs along with its commercial and sexual competitions. Brian Gibbons's *Jacobean City Comedy* takes traditional estates moralities plays, interludes, and complaints that attacked abuses of the commonwealth to be formative for the later, sophisticated subgenre. Gibbons defines the genre by its satiric tone, urban setting, characters, and incidents, especially the "lazzi" episodes of trickery from Italian commedia dell'arte. Then, following L. C. Knights's *Drama and Society in the Age of Jonson*, Gibbons allows city comedies a moral more than an economic view of moneylending as usury: extortions from the gentry and nobility signify the mortal sin avarice. And he sets a political background of distrust in James's promotion and extension of divine monarchical right. Finally he employs the genre for criticism of the city comedies written by Marston, Jonson, especially *Volpone*, and Thomas Middleton, especially *The Phoenix*, *A Mad World My Masters*, *Your Five Gallants*, *Michaelmas Term*, and *A Trick to Catch the Old One*, then for their later plays. Description of the generic characteristics of city comedy was set by Alexander Leggatt in *Citizen Comedy in the Age of Shakespeare*. Leggatt generally accepts Gibbons's terms, substituting new comedy's love and economic intrigues for the *lazzi* and ignoring political views. Mainly he establishes a generic criticism of city comedy by focusing on the characteristics of the form rather than on those of dramatists. He thereby enlarges the number of prominent playwrights and plays, including all of the *Ho* collaborations, William Haughton's founding *Englishmen for My Money*, Lording Barry's *Ram Alley*, and Edward Sharpham's *The Fleer* and *Cupid's Whirligig.* Moreover, he extends Harbage's chronological range to include Caroline drama. His generic reformulation concentrates on a presentation of urban society as those interactions between citizens and gentry, and it insists that the central common factor is the competition over the gain and control of wealth and women. Thus he establishes such set characters as the citizen hero and usurer, the prodigal, the chaste maid, wife, and whore, and various scenarios for the intrigues over money, land, women, and adultery; then he maintains a primary interest in the multitudinous variations and deployments of these types and situations. Genre criticism was consolidated when, in *The City Staged: Jacobean Comedy, 1603–1613*, Theodore B. Leinwand restored the city comedies' relations to their own time through economics, affirming both our connotation of economics as business and theirs as household.

Even as some critics were reformulating generic characterizations of city comedy and extending its bounds, others began to consider London's preeminence and to claim that the city became the dominant emblem of England's transformation into a nation. Harbage's problem plays were becoming not the antithesis but rather a mirror and a stimulus of England's developing nationhood. In 1985 Gail Kern Paster's *The Idea of the City in the Age of Shakespeare* paid heed to the development of London as the urban site of the succession of monarchs; and it focused on the enormous ambivalence roused by an increasing sense of the cosmopolitan. Paster outlined Western traditions of opposed views of an ideal community or city of God versus a predatory trap or city of man, of variety and opportunity and community versus change and destruction and chaotic competition. The city becomes figured as a matron or a whore, a time-honored trope. Then Paster employs the problem plays' depictions of strife and predation that partake little of commerce or community as counters to an ideal urbanity. Douglas Bruster's 1992 *Drama and the Market in the Age of Shakespeare* presented further problems and possibilities. He examined the simultaneous institutional establishments of commerce in the exchanges and of drama in the theaters as contributors to a burgeoning marketplace or nascent proto-capitalism. Concentrating on the problem comedies' social and moral themes, Bruster posits that the London setting is less important in itself than as a site for the presentation of the materiality and commodification of culture. He suggests that explanations of an interrelated set of questions culminate in material culture becoming an index of social as well as economic interchange and mobility, then an index of identity: why can "city comedy" be situated in other commercial centers in Europe and not just in London, why in "city comedy" do London landmarks appear in other cities, why did objects of use and fashion accrue importance and proliferate through city comedies, why does the conflux of sexuality and money persistently dominate, why do these often take the form of an obsessive preoccupation with cuckoldry and prostitution? Increasing interest in the theory of spatialization has drawn further attention to sites that can serve to map economic, sociological, and psychological functions in a changing London.[7] For instance, Janette Dillon's *Theatre, Court and City, 1595–1610* analyzes shifting moral and social evaluations in masques, plays, and documents that exploit the setting of the New Exchange with its socially and economically charged conception, design, construction, and promotion by Robert Cecil, Lord Salisbury.

The poles of desire and repulsion, attraction and threat in urban and material commerce, of morality and immorality, of integral and alien, of city and country, accrued ever more to London. Simultaneously London was coming to represent England more and the monarch to represent it less, just as Elizabeth was dying and James acceding. Abetting both of these movements, problem plays were becoming dominant in English drama. So the perspective provided by Benedict Anderson's global and theoretical *Imagined Communities* and Richard Helgerson's specifically English and applied *Forms of Nationhood* has become the major focus of studies of the problem plays: nationalism as a sense of identity distinct from loyalty to a sovereign emerged out of such overlapping conflicts. For recent critics the problem comedies bring into focus the competitions and contentions that were forging a nation as London was being made a synecdoche of nascent English nationality. In this respect, problem plays succeed history plays in helping determine what constituted England, perhaps a United Kingdom, prepared for by Elizabeth Tudor and promoted by James Stuart. Emma Smith supplies fundamental premises for discussions about how problem plays helped produce a sense of English identity when she examines William Haughton's *Englishmen for My*

Money; or, A Woman Will Have Her Will, arguably the city comedy founding the genre. Smith's analysis demonstrates how vital were, first, the personifications of London and of England as chaste bride or wife versus foreign whore and, second, the London dialect contra the accents of aliens. In this fable three daughters remain faithful to their Englishmen and the London dialect in spite of suitors favored by their father, Dutch, Italian, and French merchants who mangle English. Not that the play is wholly jingoistic. It offers a nuanced cosmopolitanism in that the girls' father is an apparently naturalized Portuguese entrepreneur married to an Englishwoman.

The more conflicted hypothesis that problem plays helped negotiate or perform Englishness from a London standpoint appears in Jean E. Howard's discussions of two plays featuring prostitution and marriage, whorehouse and home: "Mastering the Difference in *The Dutch Courtesan*" and "Women, Foreigners, and the Regulation of Urban Space in *Westward Ho*." Howard's vision of *The Dutch Courtesan* can complicate the rudimentary paradigm of an argument between marriage and prostitution partly because the stage associated English Dolls and Molls with foreigners. Thus she expands studies of incipient nationalism into characterizations of prostitution, arguments for as well as against inevitable urban intercourse with the foreign, oppositions between national religion and sectarianism, and commerce between urban and regional. These complications get summed up less in Freevill, the machiavel who ultimately reaffirms the purity of marriage in the romantic plot than in the witty rogue of the comic plot. Coccledemoy exemplifies an Englishness maintained by libertine sexuality and prostitution in the family and by difference in religion; moreover, Coccledemoy enters into cosmopolitan intercourse with and adaptation of multiple alien roles and dialects. Howard's analysis of *Westward Ho* complicates still more the incomplete process of naturalization of the foreign through its presentation of the penetrability of urban households through commerce with whorehouses by husbands and wives, not just gallants. The Italian London merchant, who combines an excessive fear of cuckoldry by his English wife with a promotion of cuckoldry in others through his disguise as Parenthesis, the penman, threatens and restores a precarious marital fidelity. Howard argues cogently for the many kinds of intercourse, the ongoing inclusions and exclusions, that, emanating from within as well as from without, determined which contending characteristics and signs, habits and morals were coming to be considered English. She describes the inevitable, necessary and desirable, continual conflicts and negotiations in the "hybridization" of London and the forging of English national consciousness.

This history thus tells about an increasing critical and historical sense of the centrality of cosmopolitanism and commerce, interchanges of goods of all kinds physical and intellectual that Harbage considered alien, at best marginal and at worst immoral. The current subtext of our studies of early modern English problem comedies is of course our own preoccupation with urban life and its increasing dominion over rural life; it combines with our excitement over the potential political, economic, informational, social, and human gains of commerce with other cultures, and with our recognition of the multiple gender and sexual roles available. Our subtext, no less than Harbage's, is what we view as our parallels with England and London as a representative of a nascent nation, perhaps a nascent United Kingdom and empire. The opposed interpretation of this subtext includes traditions more familiar to Harbage, pitting a city commerce of pollution and degradation and role performance against a country of purity and essential identity, and fearing threats of the influence of other nations and of sexual intercourse outside of heterosexual marriage. This opposed interpretation wonders what has happened with principles, beliefs, customs supposed to constitute and signify character and nationality. Together the views ask how we gain the values of intercourse with others without giving up the values we cherish in ourselves. And the terms are long familiar from anthropological studies of the gains in power through marrying out, exogamy, with the maintenance of identity through marrying in, endogamy. What in moral or national identity can pass and what needs to remain steadfast?

Such concerns return to Harbage. For we are still asking Harbage's question about how the theater represents the nation—only our answers cannot be the same, just as our history is no longer the same. First, much of our data is different and fuller. Second, there has been a sizable increase in the number of theories about the influences on and of drama. Third, there has been a multiplication of theories throughout the human, social sciences along with an increasing contest over definitions of society, nation, personality, culture—with their interchanges. Such prominently include those from newer intellectual disciplines of sexuality, gender relations, postcolonialism, and diversity. Fourth, and inclusively, there has been an enormous increase in the domain we incorporate in theory and to a lesser extent in practice about how we are made up as individuals and as societies. In brief, there has been an increasing incorporation of the intercourse of the cosmopolitan, the city. And so Harbage's theater of the nation has perforce had to include the problem plays, come to be defined more by the very problem plays that bothered him because they dominated the stage than by those plays he preferred and promoted.

In sum, the perspectives on and attitudes toward the issues and their investigation have undergone extensive revision since Harbage surveyed the ground, primarily by way of mainly focusing on what repelled him. Issues that now seem defining cluster around various versions and levels of the endogamy-exogamy binary that poses questions about the precarious balance between maintaining the integrity of identity perceived as traditional and personal with intercourse beyond those limits necessary for expansion and an improvement in status. Personally and in the extended family, this appears in the familiar instances of cuckoldry and wittolry, the dilemma of choosing between family control and personal gain, country gentlemen and venturing merchants. The same binary poses related questions for the regional formation of nationhood between country and city, including town, between the English of London and other dialectal regions and the Scotch, the Irish, and the Welsh, and across the spectrum of beliefs affirming Christianity, with primary emphases on papism and sectarianism. Beyond the isles this binary poses questions of interrelations with other emerging nationalities, primarily with the Dutch, the Italian, the French, and the Spanish, and including the Jews and the Moors. Shakespeare's trilogy of problem plays need to assume their places among the problem plays concerned with London and England and the early 1600s. For they testify and contribute to our understanding of that time and our own. *Measure for Measure* is attentive to conflicts between justice and mercy, legitimate public versus private concerns in sexuality, appropriate influence and prohibition versus inappropriate citizen manipulation, and the necessary and inevitable exchanges and negotiations required among such conflicts in principles and practices in Vienna. *All's Well That Ends Well* focuses on the appropriateness and value of unheralded feminine aggression and manipulativeness, the balance of sociopolitical and parental concerns versus individual desires in sexual and marital choice, and the promulgation versus the testing of conventional wisdom in France and Italy. And *Troilus and Cressida* is concerned with valuations of the traditional diad of honor and love, war and lechery, and the determination of these values through mutual human persuasion in Troy.

A Ground Rhetorical

I do not, however, want to approach these problem plays, once again, primarily through such ideological, sociopolitical, psychological, and sexual perspectives. Instead, in order to help us sort out, evaluate, and generate such perspectives, I propose that we can usefully return to a more formal questioning of the predicaments and tensions, resolutions and irresolutions of these dark comedies that were modulating into tragicomedy's resolving formulae of miraculous grace and forgiveness. We can restore the perspective of formal rhetoric extended based on renewed understandings of the pervasiveness and the force of rhetorical training during the era. So through studies of *Measure for Measure*, *All's Well That Ends Well*, and *Troilus and Cressida*, I will indicate the potential of this partial perspective in which the other issues are inextricably embedded. By way of entry we can consider the tone that marks problem plays, characterize stylistic elements dark comedies commonly share.

Although no comprehensive stylistic study of the problem plays yet exists, a consensus can be gleaned from sweeping studies that take into account the satiric or sarcastic tone that mixes high and low styles blatantly, that juxtaposes rhetorical elaboration and contentious antirhetorical display ostentatiously. Critical consensus essentially extends the implications of Ben Jonson's attack on John Marston's hyperrhetorical and harsh style, an attack that reached its notorious climax in the purge of hard words administered to Crispinus in *The Poetaster* (1601). Although this scene's inordinate influence has prompted most critics to credit John Marston with the newly popular style, Marston was not practicing the style in isolation. To recall widely acknowledged stylistic traits, Jonson was a master of satiric railing and mimicry, Thomas Middleton of ironic salaciousness, George Chapman of gnarled syntax and knotted imagery. Any listing would emphasize five traits: (1) a neologistic and polysyllabic diction that collides with a vulgar, often sexual and scatological, punning diction; (2) a showy rhetorical high style of repetitions, parallels, balances, and schemes generally in verse juxtaposed against an abrupt, jarringly irregular, suggestive colloquial low style customarily in prose; (3) a density of figurative language that is involved, mixed, elliptical; (4) a frequency of brief satiric characterizations; and (5) a high incidence of sententious, analytic, and self-serving proverbs. Introductions and annotations to editions of plays critically popular and long deemed exemplary, such as Marston's *The Malcontent* (1604), Jonson's *The Alchemist* (1610), Middleton's *A Chaste Maid in Cheapside* (1613), and Chapman's *The Widow's Tears* (1604), with lesser, confirming imitative plays, such as Sharpham's *The Fleer* (1606), highlight these features.[8] Shakespeare's exemplars of this common tone would include Lucio and perhaps Pompey, Lafeu and Paroles and Lavatch, Ulysses and Thersites and Diomedes, although their tone proves to be contagious enough that it infects a whole language community.

Problem plays commonly show off one diction that offers newly coined, sometimes nonce, and polysyllabic nouns and nominalizations posed against another diction, racily colloquial, often punning, sexual and scatological. *The Malcontent* has fewer notably exalted usages than Marston's norm, but it still supplies such words as "unshale," "unhele," "conformance," "distemperance," "correspondence," "composure," "surphling," "mundifieth," "inhumed," and "sirenical." Counter to such terms are Malevole's namings, the "becco," "cornuto," "cuckold," "horned beast," or Passarello's "standings" and Maquerelle's "fallings." Other terms are unmuzzled and unleashed in this dog world when Pietro Iacomo licenses Malevole "the ragged cur" to "bespurtle all" (1.2.10–11). His dismissing curse of Bilioso is representative: "the serpigo, the strangury, an eternal, uneffectual priapism seize, thee. . . . May'st thou be a notorious wittoly pander to thine own wife, and yet get no office" (2.3.32–36). So is the fool Passarello's licentious wit with his master's lady. *The Alchemist* features canting in the elaborate jargons not only of alchemy but also of astrology, dueling, puritan preaching, and biblical exegesis. Perpetually undercutting these are the epithets that characters hurl at each other, ranging from the general "plagues" to the specific "vermin," "curs," "locusts," and "unclean birds," "cockatrice," with the perpetual sexual innuendo of suburb "captain" as pimp, or "bawdy doctor." The clashing tone might be epitomized in the "venter tripartite's" commonwealth or republic, "Doll," "doxy," "punk." Despite its nonce word "freshwoman," *A Chaste Maid in Cheapside*, as typical of Middleton, does not display neologisms, Latinate diction, or nominalizations. But it offers more than its share of his characteristic bawdry. Its salacious talk is notorious through critical introductions, ranging from the characters' names (Moll to Whorehound, Touchwood to Kix, and Underman) to the Puritans' incessant double entendres at the christening. Most lines in the play can be construed sexually, whatever their primary reference, until the pervasive referential field becomes sexual. Consider the various "risings," "standings," "lyings," and "fallings," "bouts," and on and on. *The Widow's Tears* offers a few neologisms, including the nonce word "smockage" and unusual terms such as "debauch'd perdus," "pegmas," and "blandation." And it emphasizes the contentiously interpreted "confidence," the audacious, presumptuous actions personified as a goddess, by deploying it like a refrain that resounds through the play. It notably features salacious double meanings, as when Tharsalio, who "waited" on the lady Eudora's table, proposes to "weight" her bed with his full "beastlihood," as Arsace terms his sexual activities. The punishment threatened for his boldness is being "tossed in a blanket" by household servants, which he hurls back as "in a sheet by their mistress." *The Fleer* follows its Marstonian models as far as Sharpham "his first Minerua" (246) is capable. He offers for unusual diction "celsitude," "pettilassarie," "saluberrium," "restringent," and the contrasting categories of "celestriall" and "terrestriall" knight. More prolifically, he fills the text with bawdry mustered in "weapons" and "instruments," "pins," "pens," "blades," "swords" seeking their "cases," "scabbards," and "holes"; "parts" coming into "service," as they raise their "heads" and "stand stiffly" both "inwardly" and "open"; and "tails," "yards," "pair," along with other slang.

Problem plays generally link the elaborate word selection in a showily rhetorical high style that features initial and concluding repetitions, parallels, and balances, inversions, and other schemes, most often in verse; against this style they pit a witty, customarily abrupt, just off parallel, racy, and punning colloquial prose. *The Malcontent* offers the high syntactic style when Altofront appears early as the deposed and late as the restored duke of Genoa. This is in contrast to his disjunctive curt, curse-interrupted diatribes as Malevole. The juxtaposition is explicitly marked by the stage direction when, during his conversation with Celso, "BILIOSO *entering* MALEVOLE *shifteth his speech*" (1.4.43). The chaste duchess Maria and the ideal noble Celso exemplify the high style, as do Pietro Iacomo's courtly addresses or his elaborate narrative as the holy hermit, Aurelia's disdainful and then penitent lady, Mendoza's set speeches in praise and in blame of women. Notable exemplars of the low style besides Malevole include the bawd Maquerelle's brokerage, Machiavellian self-serving analyses, and advice; the bawdy fool Passarello's witty banter; and his sycophantic lord, Bilioso's sucking up. *The Alchemist* offers the juxtaposition Edward B. Partridge has analyzed as "the vicious style," the application of hyperbolic rhetoric in Subtle's flights of fantasy about alchemical transformations to the conversion of Jeremy the butler into the suburb captain Face or in descriptions of arcane technologies to the operations of his scams. Subtle's mimicry of the repetitive, slightly expanding plain style "this doth qualify," "this qualifies more," "this qualifies most" while accepting bribes or of casuistry in justifying counterfeiting, and Sir Epicure Mammon's rapt paeans to fancy foods and fancier sex also provide obvious examples.[9] Such ecstasies are chopped up by the sniping asides and direct assaults of Face laughing at Mammon's semi-blazon that grants prominent features of ruling European families to the whore Doll Common or at Mammon's "hopes" as "certitudes." Related are Surly's direct assaults on the Puritan abuses of religious practices to bilk others and Lovewit's concluding dismissals of the gulls. *A Chaste Maid in Cheapside* does not offer much in the way of a high style, excepting some parody in Whorehound's deathbed repentance and in elegiac memorial for Moll and Touchwood Junior. And in the latter, death's winding sheets make way for sex's wedding sheets and brothel hangings. Just so, the play's poetic lines are self-undercutting. Exemplary is Allwit's evaluations of his high living by way of serving as wittol to Whorehound: the founder "h'as maintained my house this ten years, / Not only keeps my wife, but a keeps me, / And all my family. . . . He gets me all my children . . . puts me to nothing" (1.2.16–20). Everywhere highly formulaic discourse collapses into a loose verse or low prose of punning bawdry and materialistic self-interest, such as in the debate between Tim and his Tutor over whether or not a fool is a rational animal. *The Widow's Tears* features a high style of hymns invoking Confidence and Hymen and a wedding masque juxtaposed against the taunts Tharsalio hurls at others and they turn back on him. Its emotive high style of Lysander and Cynthia's reactions to each others' moods and actions during his test of her fidelity breaks down in the new Governor of Cyprus's topsy-turvy nonsense. *The Fleer* positions high verse against low prose in the first scene. Its Altofront, the deposed Florentine Duke Antifront, employs a loose iambic pentameter with intermittent rimes; then the false high style sinks into the base prose of Malevole's counterpart, Fleer, exiled with his daughters among Londoners. Verse is restored briefly to Piso, son of the usurping duke visiting London, and to Fleer resuming status as Antifront in conclusion. Meanwhile the play is saturated with satire of London as the center of sexual commerce with whore-house, city, court, Scots, legal, and tobacco jokes. It is not insignificant that Christopher Gordon Petter has found six of the jests in the somewhat later *Conceits, Clinches, Flashes and Whimzies* (Sharpham, 196–97). Just so, much of *The*

Fleer's dialogue consists of one-liners akin to aphoristic comments, often single words or phrases set up by curt questions or observations.

Problem plays usually feature dense figuration and often mix image clusters in involved and convoluted, most often elliptical suggestiveness and allusiveness. Malevole's references to the sycophantic courtier Bilioso and the hosts of deceptive actors and actions as hypocritical churchmen in a biblical "pigeon house" and those to Genoa as a dog house or whorehouse culminate in a contempt-of-the-world speech: "This earth is the only grave and Golgotha wherein all things that live must rot; 'tis but the draught wherein the heavenly bodies discharge their corruption, the very muckhill on which the sublunary orbs cast their excrements" (4.5.107–11). *The Alchemist*'s elaboration of the language of alchemical transformations as refining the base, raw material of their gulls into gold and lesser coins is archetypal of such sustained figuration. *A Chaste Maid in Cheapside* is most often characterized by its insistent commingling of commercial and sexual imagery. Notorious lines abound, as Whorehound's venture to turn his Welsh whore into gold through her "mounts" and "runts" or his evaluation of Moll bringing in "two thousand pound in gold, / And a sweet maidenhead / Worth forty" (4.2.92–94). Tim repeatedly refers to his sister Moll as a jewel to be locked up in Venetian fashion and compares her health to wealth: "Changed? Gold into white money was never so changed, / As is my sister's colour into paleness" (5.2.21–21). The commercial-sexual image complex becomes punningly emblematic in the play's setting during Lent, when the illicit trade in "getting," including begetting, "flesh" thrives and when the country whore tricks the promoters with a basket of mutton hiding her bastard beneath. The image complex joins with voracious sexual and culinary appetite in lists of aphrodisiacs and biblical almond waters associated with the fertile Touchwood and in the gluttony over sweetmeats and drunkenness over sweet wines of the leaky Puritan vessels at the christening. *The Widow's Tears* proffers an opening verbal and visual pun on "suit" as clothing and as suing, "pursuit" and "suitable" in Tharsalio's wooing of Eudora in a threadbare cloak that conceals and then reveals the new outfit Eudora provides her victorious suitor. Most often it features the interlocking imagery of heated sexual contest and family generation carried by the translacer "ingenious," "genius," "ingender," in addition to "generate" and "generation" and various versions of "blood" and "high blood" as Tharsalio provides a new root for the old family tree by supplanting his elder brother. This imagery is supported by the "Venus" and "venerean," "Paphos" with variants, and variations of "Cyprus" that name the chief goddess and activity of the island setting. Not unexpectedly, despite plenty of running sexual ribaldry, *The Fleer* exhibits no sustained imagistic complexity.

Problem plays tend to introduce characters and sometimes to dismiss them with brief satiric portraits that are kin to the coming vogue of Theophrastian characters in Hall's *Characters of Virtues and Vices* or those by Overbury and Middleton or of Earle's *Microcosmography*. Pietro Iacomo provides the first by introducing Malevole just before his initial entry (1.2.16–30). Similarly, Face and Subtle introduce most of their gulls just before their entrances. In *A Chaste Maid in Cheapside*, Allwit gets the character introducing promoters (2.2.68–74) and the pair introducing and dismissing the Puritan gossips (3.2.58–75, 225–29). In *The Widow's Tears*, Lycus and Lysander's character of the climbing Spartan Rebus (1.2.18–34) sets up Tharsalio's combative raillery; similarly, the Captain of the Guard offers dual characters of the lord of misrule who governs Cyprus (5.1.136–55, 556–60). *The Fleer* in contrast employs the character to introduce estates satire. Fleer inveighs against England's makeup of whores and whoremongers (2.1.1–39), and he observes the exchange, with sexual commerce, of social mobility between gentleman and beggar or pimp, waiting woman and quean, husband and cuckold, lady and painter/cosmetologist, with their exchanges of wardrobe (2.1.124–34).

Problem plays are likely to focus on, many italicize or add quotation marks to highlight, an array of proverbial statements that range from highly moral advice through commonplace or witty observation to self-serving analysis. *The Malcontent* provides a profuse and wide range. Malevole alone employs them, often in strings, as moral reminders ("Fame ne'er heals, still rankles worse and worse; / Such is of uncontrolled lust the curse" [2.5.146–47]); prudential wisdom ("No vulgar seed but once may rise, and shall; / No king so huge, but 'fore he die may fall" [1.5.18–19]); mockery ("He that by any ways get riches, his means never shames him. . . . For impudency and faithlessness are the main stays to greatness" [5.2.83, 86]); and analysis ("The heart's disquiet is revenge most deep. / He that gets blood, the life of flesh but spills, / But he that breaks heart's peace, the dear soul kills" [1.3.150–52]). He thereby employs them not only in his own distinctive manner as in the first and last, but also in the modes of others: the contemptus mundi espoused by Pietro Iacomo's holy hermit; the prudent sexual politics in maintaining beauty, wealth, and a powerful lover advised by the bawd Maquerelle; the sycophancy spouted by Bilioso; and the cunning treachery counseled by the Machiavel Mendoza. *The Alchemist* is less profuse, but the aphoristic style can appear in the "ventures tripartite's" remarks about connies. Subtle offers an expanded aphorism to Mammon, who wants the philosophers' stone to supplant Nature: "when art, / Who's but a step-dame, shall do more than She [nature] / In her best love to mankind ever could" (1.4.25–28). Despite its allusion to Cato's textbook of moral maxims (4.1.255), *A Chaste Maid in Cheapside* employs few proverbs apart from adding occasional bawdry or mockery. Thus when Yellowhammer notes that "As there is no woman made without a flaw, your purest lawns have frays, and cambrics bracks," his wife, Maudlin, adds, "But 'tis a husband solders up all cracks" (1.1.29–31). Touchwood Junior proposes a mocking poesy for the ring he orders from Yellowhammer for Moll: "Love that's wise, blinds parents eyes" (1.1.200; 3.1.46–47). *The Widow's Tears* calls attention to its dependence on proverbs when Tharsalio responds, "I am bound to that by the proverb, madam," to Eudora's early insult, "Love me? Love my dog" (1.2.76–77). And he offers them to explain his confidence in his own Machiavellian observations against his sister-in-law's charge of cynicism caught from Italian air: "No, sister, it hath refin'd my senses, and made me see with clear eyes, and to judge of objects as they truly are, not as they seem, and through their mask to discern the true face of things" (1.1.132–35). He also uses them to exhort himself ("He's a shallow gamester that for one displeasing cast gives up so fair a game for lost" [2.3.13–15]) and to bolster his confidence in the potent fused drives of strife and sexuality ("Have you not heard this principle, 'All things by strife engender'?" [1.2.190–91]). *The Fleer*'s aphorisms come infrequently, usually in the play's characteristic imitative applications to bawdry. It offers that "*misshapen stuffe, / Is of behauiour boystrous and rough*" (1.3.13–14) and that the multiply punning whores "are no prouerbe breakers: beware the buyer say they, you shall haue enough for your money, if halfe will not serue your turne take the whole; measure by your own yard, you shal haue Winchester measure" (2.1.31–34). And it observes that "want and pride are two notorious bawdes: want makes the noblest creature sell her soule for golde, and pride doth make the gallants stoope to lust" (3.2.36–38).

Inside this common tonal community, my study questions each of Shakespeare's problem plays by taking interest in a relatively small issue and tracing its patterns as they extend through ever larger concentric concerns. First comes the figure chiasmus, one of Shakespeare's employments of the ostentatious figures featured in problem plays: How did Shakespeare deploy chiasmus generally, specifically in two contrasting scenes in *2 Henry IV*, and most pervasively and powerfully in *Measure for Measure*? Next appear dual notions of proverbial sayings and their employment in marked contrast to their notable uses of passing on oral wisdom and stimulating thought: How did characters use aphorisms along with other figurations such as recurring images to challenge, to argue and duel with, and to entrap other characters in the sexual, family, and social contests of wit and manipulation that form the plots of *All's Well That Ends Well*? Finally drawing attention are the rhetorical styles of three wits who communicate with others in ways that engage appreciation in an audience so that audience joins with them: How do Ulysses, Pandarus, and Thersites shrewdly and wittily employ talk to affirm values and manipulate others in *Troilus and Cressida*? And how does the Trojan council epitomize these styles and demonstrate rational, emotional, and ethical appeals fundamental to rhetorical analysis?

3

Chiasmus, Justice, and Mercy, *Measure for Measure*

Chiasmus, Antimetabole, Commutatio, Permutatio, Counterchange:

"Ye haue a figure which takes a couple of words to play with in a verse, and by making them to chaunge and shift one into others place they do very pretily exchange and shift the sence."

"'tis true 'tis pity, And pity 'tis, 'tis true—a foolish figure."

"Thanks, Rosencrantz and gentle Guildenstern. Thanks, Guildenstern and gentle Rosencrantz."

"I 'pretty' and my saying 'apt'? Or I 'apt' and my saying 'pretty'"?

"The use serueth properlie to praise, dispraise, to distinguish, but most commonly to confute by the inuersion of the sentence."

"The goodness that is cheap in beauty makes beauty brief in goodness."

"That we were all as some would seem to be— / Free from our faults, or faults from seeming free."

"And let the subject see, to make them know / That outward courtesies would fain proclaim / Favours that keep within."

"Ignominy in ransom and free pardon / Are of two houses; lawful mercy / Is nothing kin to foul redemption."

There is an enormous difference in mental travail between passing through the facile reversible chiasmus of pleonasm, virtual identity, or opposition and parsing the complex, conflicted, multiple relationships that chiasmus can demand.[1] English Renaissance rhetorician George Puttenham captures the figure's easy showiness in his evaluation that chiasmus can "very pretily exchange and shift the sence." In the three memorable examples of chiasmus from *Hamlet* and *Love's Labour's Lost*, Shakespeare exemplifies its facile wittiness. But the contemporary Henry Peacham complicates Puttenham's assessment when he includes among the uses of chiasmus "to distinguish, but most commonly to confute by the inuersion of the sentence." Peacham indicates the work that can be involved in processing chiasmus: its facile "exchange" and "shift" can require us to stop short for being "confuted" and then have to redefine the terms and rethink the relationships between them in "inversion." The problem play *Measure for Measure* provides examples of chiasmus that compel us to stop, to puzzle over definitions and relationships, to focus on difficulties—not merely on the definitions, the omissions, the substitutions, but especially on the complex relationships suggested far beyond simple identity, opposition, and substitution involved in straightforward exchanges. These complications compel us to ask further questions: In what ways can this figure be used? In what ways did Shakespeare use the scheme? And what are the consequences? What can chiasmus do for fun, for memorable aphorism, for complex thought such as analyzing the relationship of justice to mercy? What makes the figure apt for a problem play?

The kind of linguistic-rhetorical study practiced by Sister Miriam Joseph in creating an anatomy and catalog (*Shakespeare's Use of the Arts of Language*) and by M. M. Mahood in examining the dramatic effects of punning (*Shakespeare's Wordplay*) has undergone revival and revision. Keir Elam creates elaborate analyses of staged rhetoric in *Shakespeare's Universe of Discourse: Language-Games in the Comedies*, and Patricia Parker intensifies and expands punning into cultural criticism in *Shakespeare from the Margins: Language, Culture, Context*. Aiming at a different goal from theirs, I apply similar techniques to a relatively overlooked but intriguing scheme so as to suggest that in analyses and interpretations critics could profitably pay the kind of heed to schemes that we already do to tropes.[2] To this end I consider first some of the ways chiasmus has been employed. Moving from simple to complex uses, from traditional to recent analyses with familiar illustrations, I focus on analyses of examples throughout Shakespeare. For more sustained, detailed consideration, I look next at one relatively straightforward application of how the scheme reinforces the presentation of justice in *2 Henry IV*. Then I turn attention to a question that makes more demands, offers more intricate difficulties, and promises greater potential: What is chiasmus, a so-called mere figure of words, doing in *Measure for Measure*, a play in which Shakespeare employs it extensively and wherein it insistently requires that we focus on the complex difficulties in multiple relationships that have troubled critics for generations and that are supposed to be governed by the relationship between justice and mercy? To conclude I suggest that the chiasmic formulation of prominent issues in social, political, sexual, theological, and legal relationships in *Measure for Measure* makes a crucial contribution to posing difficulties in ways that intrigue us into attempting to negotiate them but that ultimately frustrate our attempts to do so. Not only have our proposed solutions proved to be unsatisfying, they must remain unsatisfied. For chiasmus is one of the complex, ostentatious rhetorical figures that lends itself to the expression of problems, one rhetorical earmark of the dominant cluster of plays that marked the transition from Elizabethan to Jacobean, precisely because chiasmus compels us to measure the intractability of problems.

X: Memorability, Reversibility, Opposition, Complexity

Polonius demonstrates how chiasmus can be used primarily for display when, artlessly, he proposes to seek "the cause of this effect—/ Or rather say 'the cause of this *defect*,' / For this effect defective comes by cause. / Thus it remains, and the remainder thus" (2.2.102–5). He dresses out his doubled chiasmus in the sententious, pointed, or curt style and various forms of correction and punning. Such witty display and joking likely provide the primary motive in Shakespeare's most extensive use of the figure. Just as Dr. Mardy Grothe's *Never Let a Fool Kiss You or a Kiss Fool You* and her Web site (*http://www.chiasmus.com/mailinglistarchives.html*) feature comedians and media pundits, so Shakespeare uses chiasmus most obviously for attractive comic wit. Sister Miriam Joseph calls attention to Shakespeare's typical show of appreciation amidst verbal sparring in *Twelfth Night* (81). There, when Cesario tries to correct Feste, Feste, a prolific purveyor of chiasmus, congratulates himself: "So thou mayst say the king lies by a beggar if a beggar dwell near him, or the church stands by thy tabor if thy tabor stand by the church". . . . "A sentence is but a cheverel glove to a good wit, how quickly the wrong side may be turned outward" (3.1.7–12). Likewise Keir Elam points to how, in *Love's Labour's Lost*, Mote expresses exorbitant appreciation of his own witty usage of the figure by repeating it (254): "These betray nice wenches that would be betrayed without these, and make them men of note—do you note, *men*" (3.1.17–19). Elam also points to how Antipholus of Syracuse exhibits his clout and trickery in *The Comedy of Errors* when he parries Dromio of Syracuse's sarcastic thanks for a beating (256), "for this something that you gave me for nothing": "I'll make amends next, to give you nothing for something" (2.2.50–53).

Along with display, memorability proves a primary motive for chiasmus in uses ranging from aphorisms to advertisements. So Quintilian's popular example "I do not live to eat, but eat to live" (9.3.85). Or the New Testament's "For the children ought not to lay up for the parents, but the parents for the children" (2 Cor. 12:14). Or advertising's "You can take Salem out of the country, but you can't take the country out of Salem." Or politics' John Fitzgerald Kennedy's "Ask not what your country can do for you. Ask what you can do for your country." Aphoristic memorability is what Sister Miriam Joseph particularly notes in Shakespeare's employment of the figure (81–82), for instance, in "Remember March, the ides of March, remember" (*Julius Caesar* 4.2.70). It is useful for summing up practical wisdom, as in the Duke's reply to Orlando's demand for food in *As You Like It*, "Your gentleness shall force / More than your force move us to gentleness" (2.7.101–2). Or it can sum up a situation, as in Hamlet's "Heaven hath pleased it so / To punish me with this, and this with me, / That I must be their scourge and minister" (3.4.157–59) after he kills Polonius.

Few rhetoricians discuss or exemplify the simplest use of chiasmus—repetitive tautology or identity. An important exception is Jeanne Fahnestock, who analyzes this use in her anatomy of the definitions, history, and functions of antimetabole for logic tests and arguments in *Rhetorical Figures in Science* (122–55).[3] Drawing on Aristotle's treatise on dialectic more than on his rhetoric, Fahnestock describes the figure's argumentative force in testing the convertibility of terms. She couples her description with modern treatises that emphasize how the principle of commutation proves identifying attributes and identity (131–35). In fact, she suggests, the formal structure of chiasmus encourages, at times even compels, analysis and measurement of the terms it inverts. Chiasmus serves, Fahnestock argues, as a figure that epitomizes attention to judgment. The witches' perverse identification but accurate prediction that "Fair is foul, and foul is fair" opening *Macbeth* is uncharacteristic of Shakespeare's tragedies, since he does not usually employ reversibility to test identification there. But such tests may be implicit in untangling some of his complex uses in comedies, where he does employ reversibility amply. The wordplay of the clowns in *The Two Gentlemen of Verona* offers an example. Lance describes to Speed how his staff "understands" him: "I'll but lean, and my staff under-stands me." "It stands under thee indeed." "Why, stand-under and under-stand is all one" (2.5.25–28). Frequently characters employ it for comic slights, as when Maria and Boyet of *Love's Labour's Lost* agree about Biron that "Not a word with him but a jest. / And every jest but a word" (2.1.214–15). Shakespeare uses repetitive and pleonastic chiasmus as well to suggest or to reinforce strength of belief. Brutus, for example, begs "Romans, countrymen, and lovers" in *Julius Caesar* to "Believe me for mine honour, and have respect to mine honour, that you may believe." More elaborately with equivalent substitutions he immediately adjures, "Censure me in your wisdom, and awake your senses, that you may the better judge" (3.2.14–17).

Seen in the prime examples from Quintilian, advertising, and JFK, the most frequent use of chiasmus forms an antithetical inversion rather than an identity of terms. Puttenham's frequently cited example that "We wish not peace to maintaine cruell warre, But we make warre to maintaine us in peace" (208) Shakespeare compacts to conclude *Timon of Athens* resoundingly. There Alcibiades pledges to "Make war breed peace, make peace stint war." And Peacham's description of the prominent use of chiasmus as confutation and opposition offers for its primary example "Neither was the man created for the womans sake, but the woman for the mans sake" (1 Cor. 11:9). Fahnestock observes that both rhetoricians were following the new renaissance emphasis on the figure's usefulness (129–30). This focus on antithesis Ronald H. Carpenter stresses in analyzing the strictly delineated term "antimetabole." Like Fahnestock (124–25), Carpenter suggests that chiasmic antithesis can be potent for providing a memorable persuasive climax, as when Kennedy used it to cap a series of anticipatory antitheses.[4] Aphoristic reversal provides one of Sister Miriam Joseph's important exhibits (81), Touchstone imitating Socrates in *As You Like It*: "The fool doth think he is wise, but the wise man knows himself to be a fool" (5.1.29–30). Such bear repetition and variation. In his version Touchstone merely tightens an earlier one from *Love's Labour's Lost*: "his ignorance were wise, / Where now his knowledge must prove ignorance" (2.1.101–2). Common antithesis appears among the many chiasmic expressions Henry V employs to woo, or appropriate, Catherine: "I have no strength in measure—yet a reasonable measure in strength" (5.2.132–34). Employed in sets, the antithetical scheme can reinforce a sense of conflict. A brief illustration from *Antony and Cleopatra* associates the figure with Octavia, who is supposed to cement her brother, Octavius, to Antony through a marital exchange but instead becomes a ram to batter them apart. Just after her brother introduces her prospective husband with this metaphoric opposition, Antony notes in a foreshadowing chiasmus that "Her tongue will not obey her heart, nor can / Her heart inform her tongue" (3.2.48–49). On her return to Rome after the failure of the alliance, her brother greets her with a confirming, severing relational chiasmus, "You come not / Like Caesar's sister. The wife of Antony / Should have an army for an usher" (3.6.42–44).

In between, trying to bridge the breach Octavia implores Antony by exemplifying intensively the import of his chiasmus with her own. How can she pray, since begging success for one annuls success for the other and mocks her? There exists "no midway / 'Twixt these extremes at all": "Husband win, win brother / Prays and destroys the prayer" (3.4.18–20).

Besides reversals by negation or contradiction, the figure can also contrast by degree and thereby take on more shades of meaning. In *The Taming of the Shrew*'s Induction, Sly jokes that he has "no more shoes than feet—nay, sometime more feet than shoes" (Ind.2.9–10). Leonato avers "How much better is it to weep at joy than to joy at weeping" in *Much Ado about Nothing* (1.1.23–24). Even a doubting "if" can supply the linkage, as in Maria's description of Longueville in *Love's Labour's Lost*: "The only soil of his fair virtue's gloss—/ If virtue's gloss will stain with any soil" (2.1.52–53).

Thus chiasmus, like other schemes and tropes, may increase enormously in complexity. Increased complexity issues from problems rising out of circumstances that counter both simple association or identification and straightforward opposition or reversal. Because chiasmus allows for potential relationships between terms, it may test for relations between terms from different fields, as does *commutatio* in Ch. Perelman and L. Olbrechts-Tyteca's *The New Rhetoric; A Treatise on Argumentation* (427–30) and as does *antimetabole* in Group Mu's *A General Rhetoric* (124–26). Association to the degree of identification and outright opposition then become the antithetical poles of a sizable interpretive spectrum.

That chiasmus forms multiple, complex relationships is one of three points Max Nanny makes to open his discussion "Chiasmus in Literature: Ornament or Function?" (53). As Nanny suggests, chiasmus provides a quasi-spatial relationship even though it comes as a temporal relationship in language (51). So the name was formed from the Greek X, a crossing over, as between "before" and "after" or between an image and its mirroring. Sometimes rhetoricians emphasize this by placing the two terms on parallel lines and drawing arrows to form the X. The display can be particularly expressive when the spaces also refer to moral categories, as in the exchange between Biron and Longueville in *Love's Labour's Lost*:

> How low soever the matter, I hope in God for high words. 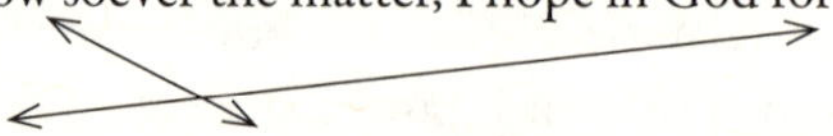
>
> A high hope for a low heaven. (1.1.189–90)

A moralizing chiasmus in *Richard II* compounds memorable temporal terms: "I wasted time, and now doth time waste me" (5.5.49). Likewise *Twelfth Night*'s Maria completes Sir Toby's chiasmus to predict the temporal consequences of Sir Andrew's prodigality: "Why he has three thousand ducats a year." "Ay, but he'll have but a year in all these ducats" (1.3.18–19). Such inversions appear profusely in *Hamlet.* After noting the closest of associations that can come about precipitously, "Grief joys, joy grieves, on slender accident," the Player King opines, "For 'tis a question left us yet to prove / Whether love lead fortune or else fortune love" (3.2.181, 184–85).

Another of Nanny's three fundamental points is that chiasmus takes on greater significance in an analytic language dependent on word order, such as English, than it possesses in a synthetic one dependent on paradigmatic conjugations and declensions. This feature links with chiasmus's potential for reversing cause and effect, a potential Fahnestock explains to be particularly useful for examining refutation and for making corrections in logic and science (150–55). A notable literary example of this feature, one with political impact, is provided by Sir John Denham's memorable and influential paired assertions opening *Coopers Hill*: Parnassus and Helicon "made not Poets, but the Poets those, / And as Courts make not Kings, but Kings the Court." Another instance of this employment of chiasmus occurs in *Paradise Lost* when Milton draws a moral by emphasizing how Satan's early scheme to produce evil out of good is reversed or corrected in Adam's late praise of God's encompassing production of good out of evil. Satan: "If then his Providence / Out of our evil seek to bring forth good, / Our labor must be to pervert that end, / And out of good still to find means of evil" (1.162–65). Adam: "O goodness infinite, goodness immense! / That all this good of evil shall produce, / And evil turn to good" (12.469–71). Such a transfer of cause and effect appears punningly in *The Merchant of Venice* when Portia, speaking of Antonio, tells Bassanio that "You should in all sense be much bound to him, / For as I hear he was much bound for you" (5.1.135–36). The difference between cause and effect is telling for Desdemona in *Othello*: "Why I should fear I know not, / Since guiltiness I know not, but yet I feel I fear" (5.2.40–41). And it is damning in Hamlet's disillusioned warning to Ophelia. In a chiasmus they form jointly, he has answered her "That if you be honest and fair, your honesty should admit no discourse to your beauty," and she has questioned, "Could beauty, my lord, have better commerce than with honesty?" Then in one he forms alone, he analyzes: "Ay, truly, for the power of beauty will sooner transform honesty from what it is to a bawd than the force of honesty can translate beauty into his likeness. This was sometime a paradox, but now the time gives it proof" (3.1.109–15).

Such tests by inversion link chiasmus to the figure *hysteron proteron*, the preposterous, the "arsie versie," the reversal of what ought by some criterion to take precedence. This figure is one on which Patricia Parker founded a series of essays culminating in "Preposterous Estates, Preposterous Events: From Late to Early Shakespeare." She exploited the resources of figuration to help loosen the boundaries of Shakespearean interpretation when she drew attention to the marginal notes where editors dispute uses of language and critics examine wordplay, when she interlinked definitions from multiple discourses and genres, and when she finally placed these meanings among cultural studies, materialist, feminist, gay, and other socially and politically inflected approaches.[5] What Parker calls "initiating" or "capping" expressions sometimes take the form of chiasmus. One such appears in the multilingual puns on salutations and farewells, epilogues and prologues during Don Armado's ridicule of Costard in *Love's Labour's Lost*, "Doth the inconsiderate take salve for *l'envoi*, and the word *l'envoi* for a salve" (3.1.68–69). Another such expression is represented in *The Taming of the Shrew*, situated amidst Parker's questioning of origins and emphasizing an inversion of generations: "Fathers commonly / Do get their children, but in this case of wooing / A child shall get a sire" (2.1.401–3).

There are yet more difficult formulations of chiasmus. Some deal with the very problem of verbal formulation itself. For instance, in a memorable scene in *The Two Gentlemen of Verona* Lance strives to understand his household's weeping through an allegory in which various props represent others: "I am the dog. No, the dog is himself, and I am the dog. O, the dog is me, and I am myself" (2.4.18–20). Similarly, a revered example comes from ancient rhetoricians, who used chiasmus to help engage in contemplation of the problems and potential of the concept *ut pictura poesis*. "A poem should be a speaking picture; a picture should be a silent poem" has stimulated centuries of analysis of the multiple relations between visual and verbal communication, relations that viewers and readers instantaneously sense from the very expression itself. More recently, Kenneth Burke has likewise employed chiasmus to stimulate thought. For example, in "you cannot have ideas without persons or persons without ideas," Burke evokes time-honored definitions of humans as speaking, abstracting, or representing animals (quoted in Fahnestock, 141).

Just as chiasmus can be extended into allegory, so it can be contracted into gnomic aphorism that begets information or simply remains puzzling. Most often in Shakespeare, because of its density or an auditor's lack of information, a gnomic chiasmus introduces a longer explanatory passage. In *The Comedy of Errors*, for instance, Egean begins the extensive exposition of his life with the claim that he was "wed / Unto a woman happy but for me, / And by me happy, had not our hap been bad" (1.1.36–38). Similarly, shortly after Gaunt responds to Richard II's "Should dying men flatter with those that live?" with "No, no, men living flatter those that die," he introduces his anatomy of Richard's failings with the observation that he is "Ill in myself to see, and in thee seeing ill" (2.1.88–89, 94). Sometimes, despite multiple proposed emendations by editors, a chiasmus remains as enigmatic as this one in *Love's Labour's Lost*: "For wisdom's sake—a word that all men love—/ Or for love's sake, a word that loves all men" (4.3.332–33). At yet other times, the difficulty of Shakespeare's chiastic figures comes not from our lack of information but from oxymora condensed in puns and inversions, as in Romeo's puling Petrarchan lament over Rosaline, "O brawling love, O loving hate" (1.1.169), or Claudio's dismayed dismissal of Hero at the aborted wedding in *Much Ado about Nothing*: "But fare thee well, most foul, most fair, farewell / Thou pure impiety and impious purity" (4.1.101–2). Sometimes, however, amplification of a Shakespearean chiasmus may occur just for humor or thematic expatiation. It is for humor, for instance, when Claudio explains a chiasmus formed jointly with Don John to tease Benedick: "Hath any man seen him at the barber's?" "No, but the barber's man hath been seen with him, and the old ornament of his cheek hath already stuffed tennis balls" (3.2.36–39). But it is for theme or characterization that auditors puzzle out Hamlet's bitter pair of chiasmic explanations to Ophelia.

Finally, besides using gnomic density, Shakespeare can complicate chiasmus by substituting terms, using various forms of punning, and playing other word games. *Love's Labour's Lost* provides numerous examples, including puns that interchange parts of speech, as when Biron opens the courtiers' poetic professions of love by comparing his love for Rosalind to the deer hunt, "They have pitched a toil; I am toiling in a pitch" (4.3.2). A more straightforward example, one to which Sister Miriam Joseph calls attention

(81), occurs in *The Merchant of Venice* when Portia, making fun of a suitor, substitutes "worst" for "worse" and "beast" for "best": "When he is best he is a little worse than a man, and when he is worst he is little better than a beast" (1.2.73–75). Similarly, in *Much Ado about Nothing*, Benedick—simultaneously providing a summation and a transition to his peroration—employs a chiasmus punning on notions of "grace": "But till all graces be in one woman, one woman shall not come in my grace" (2.3.25–26). A frequently cited example from *Love's Labour's Lost* appears when Don Armado declares that "I love not to be crossed" and Moth responds by punning on and personifying the coin: "He speaks the mere contrary—crosses love not him" (1.2.31–33). In more complicated variations on the form, Shakespeare can substitute synonyms or antonyms, as when Juliet realizes on learning Romeo's identity that her "only love" is "Too early seen unknown, and known too late" (1.5.136). More elaborate still are metonymic substitutions, as when in *The Merchant of Venice* Portia tells Nerissa aphoristically that "The brain may devise laws for the blood, but a hot temper leaps o'er a cold decree" (1.2.15–17). While the substitutions in these examples are explicit, chiasmus may even work by an implicit substitution of a term. In *King Lear*, for instance, Edgar disguised as Mad Tom just before the appearance of his blinded father aphoristically affirms that he is better off ragged and aware of being scorned than he would be were he scorned unawares since flattered for his wardrobe's display of wealth and status: "Yet better thus, and known to be contemned / Than still contemned and flattered" (4.1.1–2).

The potential complexity of chiasmus thus recommends it for the expression of problematic relationships such as that between Claudius and Gertrude or, more abstractly, that between concepts of justice and mercy. It is not insignificant that the greatest concentration of the figure in *Hamlet* (a play often associated with the other problem plays) occurs when the Player King and Queen in the Mousetrap discuss whether or not she will wed after the death of her first husband, the test Hamlet considers "wormwood" for Gertrude. That discussion begins with the Player Queen's affirmation that "Where love is great, the littlest doubts are fear: / Where little fears grow great, great love grows there" and is capped with the Player King's query, "For 'tis a question left us yet to prove / Whether love lead fortune or else fortune love" (3.2.154.1–2, 184–85). Similarly, it does not seem insignificant that, by the account of Brian Vickers, relying on J. B. Broadbent, the greatest concentration of chiasmus in Milton's *Paradise Lost* comes in book 3. For there Milton presents the discussion in heaven between the Father and Son who both exemplify and state the relationship in Christianity between law and love, God's justice and mercy.[6] Shakespeare likewise employs chiasmus to express questions about justice and mercy. Toward the end of a memorable defense of the humanity of Jews as no less than that of Christians, Shylock uses chiasmus with catechism to declare that vengeance is the rule of justice: "If a Jew wrong a Christian, what is his humility? Revenge. If a Christian wrong a Jew, what should his sufferance be by Christian example? Why, revenge" (3.1.57–59). Given these examples of how Milton and Shakespeare use chiasmus to explore the complexities of justice and mercy, there should be little surprise that chiasmus becomes a dominant figure during two important moments in *2 Henry IV* when the principle of what constitutes just rule is at stake or that the greatest concentration of chiasmus in Shakespeare appears when *Measure for Measure* compounds the same troubling problem that constitutes one center of attention in *The Merchant of Venice*—the relation of law and clemency, justice to mercy.

Justice: The Case of *2 Henry IV*

Chiasmus proves useful for presentations of justice precisely because of its reversibility and its display's conduciveness to measurement. In *2 Henry IV* Shakespeare employs it to focus Hal's choice between Falstaff and the Lord Chief Justice as his adoptive father on becoming Henry V. Here chiasmus ultimately reinforces a principle of measured and balanced rule. But the question whether Hal will be just, the prime virtue for a monarch, or willful, the mark of a tyrant, is pressed from the second scene and first confrontation of the two antagonists, when Falstaff threatens ominously. This scene introduces as well chiasmus strategically positioned so that it links to the very question of who makes an appropriate advisor to the prince. Early in the confrontation the Lord Chief Justice offers openings for a pair of chiasmi that Falstaff jokingly takes advantage of so as to reverse the intent along with the form:

> LORD CHIEF JUSTICE Your means are very slender, and your waste is great.

FALSTAFF I would it were otherwise; I would my means were greater and my waist slenderer.

LORD CHIEF JUSTICE You have misled the youthful Prince.

FALSTAFF The young Prince hath misled me. (1.2.128–33)

Toward the end of the confrontation, after Falstaff has made fun of Hal cuffing the Lord Chief Justice, the offended lord implores, "Well, God send the Prince a better companion!" Again Falstaff inverts: "God send the companion a better prince!" (1.2.181–83). But the Lord Chief Justice's "wit" has "severed" them.

The question of Hal's choice reaches its climax when the Lord Chief Justice is granted victory, not in the play's infamous rejection scene when Henry V commands the Lord Chief Justice to silence and discipline Falstaff but rather as the second of a pair of scenes occurring somewhat earlier. In the earlier of the pair, Falstaff observes an old acquaintance, the country justice Shallow, accept his servant Davy's plea to exercise favoritism and subvert justice by "countenancing" a known knave; then he schemes about how to exploit Shallow's injustice. In the later of the paired scenes, Henry V announces his choice in a display that begins with a test of the Lord Chief Justice for sentencing Hal to prison for striking the Lord Chief Justice in his "very seat of judgement" and concludes with Henry's judgment "You shall be as a father to my youth" (5.2.79–117).

Having watched Shallow and Davy, Falstaff analyzes the flagrant abuse of justice in a pair of chiastic expressions. As he contemplates telling a farce funny enough "to keep Prince Harry in continual laughter" through numerous court terms (5.1.67), Falstaff's chiastic expressions imitate wrongful elevation and leveling. Shallow's servants, "by observing him, do bear themselves like foolish justices; he, by conversing with them, is turned into a justice-like servingman" (5.1.56–58). The point of Falstaff's chiasmus is the inversion of status, for the justice unjustly considers himself above the law and wrongfully elevates his servants so they join him there. Through the figure Falstaff observes an inverted leveling of judgment and of status that overturns justice.

Having made that point, Falstaff goes on to compare master and servants to geese flocking together and transmitting diseases among themselves. Consequently, he continues, "If I had a suit to Master Shallow, I would humour his men with the imputation of being near their master; if to his men, I would curry with Master Shallow that no man could better command his servants" (5.1.60–64). Characteristically, Falstaff's tactic is to turn the failure of justice into commodity, plotting to exploit Shallow and to entertain Hal. But Falstaff's prospect of entertaining Hal as Henry V would exploit the very conditions Davy uses to exploit Justice Shallow: it levels the servant and the master by raising the servant to the status of the master and by raising them both above the law. So later that evening when he hears of the death of Henry IV, Falstaff feels confident in asserting that "The laws of England are at my commandment" and so is the Lord Chief Justice (5.3.125–26). For Falstaff believes both that the "young King is sick" for him and also that he is nearly even with the king above the law. The doubled chiasmus Falstaff employs in his analysis and his strategy lays bare the proposed interchange of inequitable roles and the discard of justice.

The scene Henry V stages for the Lord Chief Justice in view of his court turns that wrong to right. By means of doubling another chiasmus he restores the order of justice by reversing the flow Falstaff perceived. Henry's decisive turn against Falstaff's inversion of justice comes after the new king's entry to the court of brothers and retainers apprehensive about his intentions. It provides the climax to a legal lesson.

In the scene the new monarch first argues his old personal case as prince against the Lord Chief Justice. Having once jailed Hal, the jurist rightly dreads forewarnings of the new king's grudge and the need to appease Falstaff. So, in response to the king, the Lord Chief Justice features three approaches: first, recourse to a general impersonal principle in "The majesty and power of law and justice, / The image of the King whom I presented" when Hal struck him (5.2.77–78); next, recourse to a specific precedent; and third, recourse to a hypothetical case wherein the new king is to project a parallel circumstance with his son. Declaring him correct, Henry says that the Lord Chief Justice has weighed the case well and that he shall thereafter bear the insignia of his office, the balance and the sword. Then, in a chiasmus Henry sums up his decision by quotation that gives justice first and last place and the prince the intermediate role:

So shall I live to speak my father's words:
"Happy am I that have a man so bold
That dares do justice on my proper son,

And not less happy, having such a son
That would deliver up his greatness so
Into the hands of justice." (5.2.106–11)

Henry restores order under the law with hierarchical reciprocity of status and duties that, in his first scene, Falstaff had flouted "in new silk and old sack" and that, during the scenes considering Shallow and Davy that flank this one, he dreams of flouting in the new regime. In his definitive emblematic chiasmus, Hal as Henry V immediately confirms his decision for justice and order:

You did commit me,
For which I do commit into your hand
Th'unstained sword that you have used to bear. (5.2.111–13)

Simultaneously Henry V rights an ordered justice and a balanced chiasmus.

But, judged by critics' dismay over Henry V's and the Lord Chief Justice's consequent treatment of Falstaff and over Hal's reclamation as the son of the deeply disturbing Henry IV, justice does not come as easily as these scenes would make it seem. Nor does the relation of justice to mercy seem easy when posed by *Measure for Measure*.

The Case of *Measure for Measure*

Duke Vincentio's final remarks to Isabella epitomize yet one more problem in yet one more of the chiasmic formulations of problems prevalent throughout *Measure for Measure*. Judged by critical consternation, "What's mine is yours, and what is yours is mine" (5.1.530), spoken by a duke to a subject, a man to a woman, an elder to a junior, a Machiavel to an innocent, sounds to many like "What's mine is mine, and what is yours is mine." This chiasmus is not rightly reversible; it is controverted by the situation in which it is spoken. So, judged by even more critical consternation, is the always difficult relationship between justice and mercy, law and equity, the play's vexed central theme. Its critical expression comes, at the play's climactic moment, in the duke's pronouncement of judgment:

The very mercy of the law cries out
Most audible, even from his proper tongue,
'An Angelo for Claudio, death for death.'
Haste still pays haste, and leisure answers leisure;

Like doth quit like, and measure still for measure.
Then Angelo, thy fault's thus manifested,
Which, though thou wouldst deny, denies thee vantage. (5.1.399–405)

The passage is stark in its pounding parallels of *conduplicatio*, repetition of the terms—death, haste, leisure, like, measure—that reassert their identity in equal exchange. Significantly, a capping chiasmus—fault "though thou wouldst deny, denies thee vantage"—applies an indisputable principle of judgment.

Despite this decisiveness, repealed immediately afterwards, no critic has ever doubted that *Measure for Measure* creates problems—if not for his or her own allegory, then for the reception of the allegories of others. Moreover, whatever the play's proclaimed genius, judgments have it that this problem play presents a fable implausibly contrived, characters inconsistent or inconsistently perceived, language as knotty as poetic, a troubled if not discordant tone, radically multiple viewpoints, a focus that shifts midplay.[7] But the central theme of this problem play of problematic chiasmic formulations ought to be clear. The rule of justice is clear: equal treatment, equal rewards and punishments, of subjects governed under the same liberties and prohibitions. Angelo declares it: "When I that censure him do so offend, / Let mine own judgement pattern out my death, / And nothing come in partial" (2.1.29–31). The principle of equity is equally clear: clement treatment, lesser punishment, whenever the strict application of law without regard to mitigating circumstances would result in unfair penalty. As Isabella puts it, "ask your heart what it doth know / That's like my brother's fault. If it confess / A natural guiltiness, such as is his, / Let it not sound a thought upon your tongue / Against my brother's life" (2.2.140–43).[8] But the relationship between justice and mercy, legality and equity, is vexed precisely because of intervening conditions.

The two starkest presentations of the issues, those of Marc Shell and Harriett Hawkins, render obvious the utility of a figure that exhibits for analysis the reversibility of the terms supposed identical or equivalent, the oppositions posited, and the exchanges proposed. In *The End of Kinship*, Shell provides the fullest discussion of the Judaeo-Christian context of *lex talionis* requiring the measure of proposed legal, quasi-legal, licit and illicit exchanges of head for maidenhead, maidenhead for head, maidenhead for maidenhead, and head for head that *Measure for Measure* presents; he also analyzes many of the issues of the inextricable sexual, marital, and legal entanglements.[9] In her Twayne New Critical Introduction to *Measure for Measure*, Hawkins gives the most problematic presentation of the enormous range of logically irreconcilable contradictions expressed between characters and even by single characters.

Unlike its role in *2 Henry IV*, chiasmus in *Measure for Measure* does not resolve issues but instead troubles them. Here it works for irresolution, combining with other techniques that introduce greater complexities. Such are the insistently telling puns on "sense" as "good sense" versus "sensuality" ("'tis such sense / That my sense breeds with it" thinks Angelo [2.2.144–45]) and gradations in between analyzed by William Empson in "Sense in *Measure for Measure*." And such are the sexual metaphors that emerge and leak into legality when Angelo defends strict enforcement of the edict against extramarital sex in order to block future sins from being "new conceived" and thereby initiating their "progress to be hatched and born" (2.2.95–101). In *Measure for Measure* chiasmus by way of inversion so lays bare the identity and association, opposition, and gradation in exchanges that we stop and measure the propositions at issue. What is more, its formulations so complicate the propositions by means of puns, substitutions, deletions, and extensions that they anatomize the complex multiple contentions entailed in judgments. For other domains inextricably impinge on the relationships between legality and equity: the character of those judging and judged, the relative well-being of subjects and commonwealth, the moralities of sexuality and procreation, the use of subterfuge by rulers, and the distinctions between what seems and what is.

In *Measure for Measure* the characteristic role of Renaissance wit—assembling data by association, correspondence, or identification—appears forcefully formulated by chiasmus. Wit shows up as a joke about identification in the punning salutation between the malaprop constable Elbow and the Duke disguised as a friar. Elbow: "Bless you, good father friar." The Duke: "And you, good brother father" (3.1.268–69). Not insignificantly, this abrupt chiasmus comes in the middle of the third act. Set inside the prison, this act offers the highest concentration of chiasmus, a signal that it serves as a fulcrum of problems. Shortly after the exchange with Elbow, the Duke/Friar uses the figure to identify immorality and its consequences to Elbow's antagonist, the pimp Pompey: "If the devil have given thee proofs for sin, / Thou wilt prove his" (3.1.285–86). Similarly the Provost employs the scheme to identify drunkenness, "Drunk many times a day, if not many days entirely drunk" (4.2.139). Chiasmus does far more than define morality. According to the Duke/Friar, news becomes the repetitious evidence of society's instability: "This news is old enough, yet it is every day's news" (3.1.454–55). Definitions by chiasmus, as in this punning gnome, frequently complicate and trouble. The executioner Abhorson's cryptic claim that his occupation constitutes an honorable guild, a mystery, because "Every true man's apparel fits your thief" requires Pompey's chiastic explication: "If it be too little for your thief, your true man thinks it big enough. If it be too big for your thief, your thief thinks it little enough" (4.2.34–37). As both Lever and Eccles suggest, Pompey understands that hangmen who inherit the suits of victims as professional payment thereby fit with the guild of tailors and so constitute a craft, a mystery understandable in the double meaning of "big enough" in size and value.[10] Chiasmus defines *Measure for Measure* in ways that at the same time mysteriously trouble.

Nowhere does chiasmus form identifications in more troubling ways than in characterizations, particularly those of Angelo, Duke Vincentio, and Isabella. In a mirroring chiasmus, Angelo opens his confession of a divided will after his fall and before his treacherous offer of Claudio's head for Isabella's maidenhead. While his prayer mouths oaths to God, his will focuses on his desires: "When I would pray and think, I think and pray / To several subjects" (2.4.1–2). Likewise, during the central prison scene, a pairing of chiasmi opens a bifurcated response to the Duke. First as Friar, confronting accusations of the Duke by his declared intimate Lucio, he stipulates the necessity of a favorable evaluation: "Love talks with better knowledge, and knowledge with dearer love" (3.1.388–89). Thus praise of the Duke's dedication to the welfare of Vienna is compromised when his deputy Escalus, led on by the Duke/Friar's question, characterizes him as "Rather rejoicing to see another merry than merry at anything which professed to make him rejoice" (3.1.459–60).

Isabella is characterized in another pair of chiasmi, one by the Duke and another by herself during their prison conference. In one the Duke/Friar employs a chiasmus so elliptical as to require his own elaboration—and ever after, explication by editors: "The goodness that is cheap in beauty makes beauty brief in goodness; but grace, being the soul of your complexion, shall keep the body of it ever fair" (3.1.182–84). His chiasmic dispraise of short-lived physical attraction given by nature sets up his praise of Isabella's integrity of soul granted and sustained by God. In the second Isabella, responding to the request to help Angelo's betrothed Mariana play the bed trick, vows to maintain her soul's integrity in her actions: "I have spirit to do anything that appears not foul in the truth of my spirit" (3.1.203–4). With its pun between the first and last "spirit," Isabella's variation of chiasmus defines her pure will in action. At the same time, however, it nominates her as the judge of the foulness or truth opposed through these middle terms. The chiasmus precisely lays bare Isabella's self-possessed faith in her own spiritual insights, which can be lauded as integrity, deplored as willful self-ignorance, or questioned as fearful overcompensation. All of these views receive ample testimony in the variorum compilation of judgments of her. Moreover, beginning and ending with Isabella's "spirit," this chiasmic formulation compels our consideration of an affirmation of soul and will that in the conclusion she denies. For in begging forgiveness for Angelo she pleads that "His act did not o'ertake his bad intent / And must be buried but as an intent / That perished by the way" (5.1.443–45).

In *Measure for Measure* identifications and associations formed by chiasmus usually lead to problems. A chiasmic pairing that opens the next scene, where Mariana is listening to a boy sing, indicates how opposed motives and ends can rise from the same topic. Mariana describes her reaction to the music in yet another chiasmus formed with antonyms, "My mirth it much displeased, but pleased my woe" (4.1.13). The Duke/Friar responds aphoristically with another chiasmus: "music oft hath such a charm / To make bad good, and good provoke to harm" (4.1.14–15). A similar potential for treacherous motives and evil ends compels Angelo's anguished chiasmus when he first enters into temptation: "O cunning enemy, that, to catch a saint, / With saints dost bait thy hook!" (2.2.184–85).

During the Renaissance judgment's evaluations of differences were inextricably linked to wit's associations. Just so, in *Measure for Measure* judgment appears in potent chiasmic formulations that lay bare for analysis the commensurability of proposed substitutions and exchanges. Sometimes, as when there is mutuality, the exchange is commensurable. For instance, when Juliet confesses in response to the Duke/Friar's interrogation, their joint chiasmus displays the exchange. He: "Love you the man that wronged you?" She: "Yes, as I love the woman that wronged him" (2.3.26–27). Even though he claims that Juliet's sin was greater, because the Duke/Friar recognizes a mutual offence, the chiasmic reversal of the parties corroborates just balance to the degree of virtual identity, as in betrothal and marriage. Sometimes, however, the exchange is questionable. For example, Angelo expresses the dubious notion, based on an analogy to counterfeiting coins, that creating an illegitimate life commits an offence commensurate to destroying a legitimate one. In terms of authorization, humans committing both acts do wrongfully play God. But Angelo expresses the premise in a variation on chiasmus so complex that it slows us into thinking through the proposed exchange and realizing it falsifies the previous analogy because of its very punning on "false": "'Tis all as easy / Falsely to take away a life true made / As to put metal in restrained moulds, / To make a false one" (2.4.46–49).

Some of the play's earliest chiasmic formulations state precisely the difficulties that motivate both equity and also a Christian precedent for equity. When Angelo and Escalus first discuss their commission Escalus laments that Angelo sentences Claudio to a beheading rather than to a wedding with Juliet for the common offense of taking her maidenhead before marriage: "Well, heaven forgive him, and forgive us all! / Some rise by sin, and some by virtue fall" (2.1.37–38). Escalus's pairing sums up the need for mercy, and its sanction: forgiveness must arise because inexplicably as well as inevitably virtue can fail and evil succeed; both good and ill are condemned, unless there is merciful intervention by God, and in imitation by a judge. This variation of chiasmus depends on the substitution of outside antonyms "rise"/"fall" and inside ones "sin"/"virtue," antonyms that by inversion halt us into examining a wrongful exchange that needs to be righted. Similarly, Isabella makes a parallel argument for Angelo's clemency on her brother. Her doubled chiasmus focuses our attention on mercy by a simultaneous pair of ploys. She presents the golden rule—sympathetic identification and reflective reciprocity—and formally represents that identification and exchange of terms, but she excepts Angelo: "If he had been as you and you as he, / You would have slipped like him, but he, like you, / Would not have been so stern" (2.2.66–68). The effect reverses Angelo's decision.

Where justice and mercy are concerned, the exchanges proposed arouse outright oppositions and create difficult problems for claims of identity that are wrong and for claims of value that are incommensurate. Among the most compelling wrongs is Angelo's vicious claim that accepting Isabella's sex in exchange for Claudio's life is identical to the virtue clemency. When Angelo tries to trap Isabella, she not only denies the equivalence between the loss of a nun's virginity and the loss of a man's life, but also the very exchange. She denies the exchange by way of a chiasmus made of synonymous terms: "Ignominy in ransom and free pardon / Are of two different houses; lawful mercy / Is nothing kin to foul redemption" (2.4. 112–14). In another chiasmus, the Duke/Friar, anticipating the release of Claudio after the bed trick, confirms her denial. So displaying and measuring differences as to discover antithesis and Angelo's sin, this exchange would countenance the sinner for love of the sin rather than forgive the sinner despite the sin: "When vice makes mercy, mercy's so extended / That for the fault's love is th'offender friended" (4.2.104–5).

In another set of proposed exchanges, the difficulty comes from the lack of assurance about the values claimed for the terms. Claudio's physical fears of an exchange based on the grace of life everlasting promised in Matthew 16:25 lead to his faltering and to an impasse. He affirms the paradox rightly as a chiasmus: "To sue to live, I find I seek to die, / And seeking death, find life" (3.1.42–43). But when he learns from Isabella that she can purchase his head with her maidenhead, his resolve to choose death in exchange for life fails because he dreads physical death. In contrast, as Isabella refuses to accept the exchange of her chastity for her brother's life, she expresses twice over as chiasmus her unwavering integrity as the novitiate nun and bride of Christ and also her belief in the promised paradox. In the first, simpler, chiasmus, one contemplating the damning pollution of compelled bribery after Angelo's attempt to trap her, she denies that the exchange of her everlasting soul is commensurable with her brother's mortal physical life: "Then Isabel live chaste, and brother die: / More than our brother is our chastity" (2.4.184–85). In the second, more complex variation of chiasmus, she claims that her potential son's illegitimate entry into life would exact a sacrifice far greater than her brother's legally forfeited life: "I had rather my brother die by the law than my son should be unlawfully born" (3.1.189–90). Here, by laying out for examination the proposed double exchange and crossing the proposed internal exchange of lawful and unlawful, Isabella refuses to save her brother's legal forfeiture by her potential illegal bastard. Two lives in place of the loss of one might seem a good trade. But, since by weighing the crucial internal exchange she realizes that acceptance would destroy her son's integrity and her own, she finds the exchange wanting, incommensurable. In both of these chiastic replies Isabella affirms her Christian faith and pledges her soul to the Christian promise Claudio doubts. But as with the

Duke/Friar's immediately preceding chiasmus in praise of her lasting beauty in goodness and her own subsequent avowal of her integrity of spirit in action, these remain vulnerable to charges of egoism and inconsistency.

Compelling questions about the weighing and balancing of the antitheses and exchanges required by the interactions of law and equity appear in chiasmic forms through the fifth act, the second-greatest concentration of the figure and the climactic trial scene in *Measure for Measure*. In a chiasmus varied in substitution and extended in image, the Duke as the Friar once more bears witness to his disgust at the corruption of Vienna because laws that proscribe such corruption are ignored: "laws for all faults, / But faults so countenanced that the strong statutes / Stand like the forfeits in a barber's shop" (5.1.313–15). His worry that the law has been "as much in mock as mark" recalls his questionable motive for first disappearing, his need for others to enforce the law in the face of his incapacity do so himself. Doubts about the Duke's justice get reinforced in a chiasmus during Lucio's protest near the end of the play: "Your highness said even now I made you a duke; good my lord, do not recompense me in making me a cuckold" (5.1.509–10). The question about the Duke's justice, the chief question about any ruler, appears as a chiasmus that directly balances the exchange and suggests that the Duke's subsequent punishment of Lucio for jesting slander is unfair.

By presenting associations and identities that lay open definitions, and antitheses and commensurabilities that lay out exchanges, chiasmus focuses our attention on many problems adjudicating strict applications of law and grants of clemency in *Measure for Measure*. The figure further directs our attention to complex problems caused by the inevitable overlaps among domains of concern that from about 1980 have dominated criticism. Since 1979, when Darryl Gless consolidated a mass of criticism and posited an overarching Christian allegory of sermon-on-the-mount charity, criticism has exhibited ever greater interest in two areas: sexual and gender issues addressed primarily by psychoanalytic criticism, following directions set by Richard P. Wheeler's *Shakespeare's Development and the Problem Comedies: Turn and Counter-Turn*; and the social and political impingement on personal and family morality generally based on Foucauldian analyses, as urged by Jonathan Dollimore's "Transgression and Surveillance in *Measure for Measure*," Leonard Tennenhouse's "Family Rites; City Comedy, Romance, and the Strategies of Patriarchalism," and Richard Wilson's "Prince of Darkness: Foucault's Shakespeare."[11] In *Measure for Measure* the social and political theme is initially signaled by chiasmic display of the play's insistence on inseparable public and personal motives. In the play's first chiasmus the Duke tells Angelo that "Thyself and thy belongings / Are not thine own so proper as to waste / Thyself upon thy virtues, they on thee" (1.1.29–31). Then he adds the illuminating New Testament monitory image to not hide one's candle under a bushel (Matt. 5:14–16). During the crucial third act the interlock of public and personal is enforced by one chiasmus and made problematic by another. In the first, amidst a cluster of three chiasmi, Elbow asserts that Angelo has selected the punishment of personal sexual deviance as the emblem of public reformation: "The deputy cannot abide a whoremaster. If he be a whoremonger and comes before him, he were as good go a mile on his errand" (3.1.290–91). But in a second chiasmus, one gnomic in its substitutions and commercial analogy, the Duke/Friar confesses that the paucity of personal honesty and loyalty threatens even partnerships and threatens much more social incorporation: "There is scarce truth enough alive to make societies secure, but security enough to make fellowships accursed" (3.1.451–54).

There exists a long heritage, demonstrated in Debora Kuller Shuger's exploration of political theories that frame *Measure for Measure*, of state enforcement of personal sexual moralities in recognition that sexual desires can be transmitted as social disorders and in consequence that sexual prohibitions ought to be legislated for a perceived social good or a given morality.[12] Such a public enforcement of private values has nevertheless, and especially since the 1960s' sexual liberation, caused more critical consternation than any other aspect of *Measure for Measure*. The figure chiasmus focuses this vexed issue by laying bare for examination its problems of identification and commensurability. Chiasmus introduces the very topic through banter about contracting socially transmitted diseases. "Do I speak feelingly now?" a gentleman asks Lucio, the waggish spokesman for licentiousness. "I think thou dost, and indeed with most painful feeling of thy speech," Lucio replies, completing the crossover (1.2.32–34). Both public and private positions are sustained in lines already noticed. Whereas Juliet's affirmation of mutual love (2.3.26–27) is less than acceptable to the Duke/Friar, Isabella's affirmation of the law's condemnation of Claudio and refusal of illegitimacy (3.1.189–90) wins his applause. But Isabella's stance may be accused of rigid and excessive communal regulation since she regards as too lenient the nunnery's rules regarding how votarists may, rarely, meet and speak with men. They may meet them only in the prioress's presence, and "Then if you speak, you must not show your face; / Or if you show your face, you must not speak" (1.4.12–13). Exacerbated by the collective opinion of Lucio, Pompey, and the Provost that premarital coupling hardly violates the Viennese norm, uneasiness builds over condemnation of a mutually generative betrothed couple. A paired chiasmus accentuates one outrageous inequity: whereas the Duke condones the bed trick, which seals an old betrothal but lacks mutual consent, he condemns the union of Claudio and Juliet despite their mutual love. By the use of sexual puns and nameless imputations, Mariana acknowledges the disparity in the Duke's judgments when, gnomically, she testifies for and against Angelo in the climactic trial scene: "I have known my husband, yet my husband / Knows not that ever he knew me" (5.1.184–85). Resolving the mystery by identifying Angelo as her husband, her chiasmic expression of the bed trick is tortuously enigmatic: Angelo "thinks he knows that he ne'er knew my body, / But knows, he thinks, that he knows Isabel's" (5.1.198–99). Mariana's chiasmus demands more than linguistic and semiotic parsing; it demands as well a concomitant situational and social analysis.

Because the Duke, the principal guardian of justice and equity hearing the case, had arranged the bed trick, whether for public or private good, Mariana's statement also raises other questions. It calls into question even a divine ruler's right or duty to go beyond equity as well as legality in manipulating subjects for the good of the state. That is, such an act of extension that potentially trespasses against both areas of righteousness makes subjects worry about where to situate the Duke between virtuous Machiavellian governor to be admired as in *Basilikon Doron* (Lever, xlviii–l) and vicious Machiavellian politician popular on stage.[13] That is, the problem focused by chiasmi replicates that presented by the protagonists of *The Malcontent*, *The Fleer*, and others of the disguised prince subset of problem plays surrounding *Measure for Measure*, such as Middleton's *The Phoenix* and Marston's *The Fawn*. The hedged chiasmus affirming the Duke's central purpose as the happiness of his subjects (3.1.459–60) tends toward good governance. But in an earlier chiasmus, the Duke implicates himself in sleazy manipulation. Complicated by substitution of "nature" for "name," his statement asserts his purpose to employ an agent to regain by sneak attack the public order he failed to maintain and, by the agent's taking the blame for the aggression, to permit him to preserve his own popularity. He has "imposed the office" on Angelo, "Who may in th'ambush of my name strike home, / And yet my nature never in the fight / T'allow in slander" (1.3.40–43).

In *Measure for Measure* chiasmic expressions repeatedly display and invert one central difficulty so as to anatomize the relationship of judgment and mercy, legality and clemency that the play requires: distinguishing seeming from being, appearance from fact and value, among the myriads of competing associations, antitheses, exchanges, and overlaps of domain. In the first of these chiasmic expressions, Isabella characterizes Angelo's oath affirming his vicious proposal. The chiasmus is complicated, for her response inverts his implicit claim of upright moral character and parallels the crucial "purpose" strategically. Whereas his initiation of the chiasmus is supposed to lend credence to his oath in the middle, hers devalues him in the conclusion: "Believe me, on mine honour, / My words express my purpose." "Ha, little honour to be much believed, / And most pernicious purpose! Seeming, seeming!" (2.4.148–50). The same seeming/being theme is sustained by the Duke/Friar during the central prison scene. There he observes the discrepancy between Angelo's magistracy and his personal behavior: "That we were all as some would seem to be—/ Free from our faults, or faults from seeming free" (3.1.293–94). In the trial scene the figure and theme of seeming/being, outer/inner, public/private reach a climax of concentration and complexity. There the Duke stages a subterfuge entrapping Angelo, taking Angelo's hand and claiming that he does so to show the populace "That outward courtesies would fain proclaim favours that keep within" (5.1.16). Trying to preclude Isabella's charge, Angelo introduces the first half of a chiasmus that Isabella completes in rebuttal and attestation. "And she will speak most bitterly and strange." "Most strange, but yet most truly," she responds (5.1.36–37). Isabella concludes this formal and thematic series with a pair of chiasmi. In the one she is expansive in describing the angelic attributes that seem to belong to Angelo versus the treacherous caitiff/villain that in fact he is: "'Tis not impossible / But one, the wicked'st caitiff on the ground, / May seem as shy, as grave, as just, as absolute, / As Angelo; even so may Angelo, / In all his dressings, characts, titles, forms, / Be an arch-villain" (5.1.52–57). In the other she is succinct in changing parts of speech. In a revealing anatomy of the sort that chiasmus compels, hers begs an interrogation to discover the truth she has just described: "let your reason serve / To make the truth appear where it seems hid, / And hide the false seems true" (5.1.65–67).

In these last quotations chiasmus calls for our scrutiny of the hypocrisy of Angelo, the point that gains more assent than any other in the play. But the figure's preponderance in *Measure for Measure* compels a more powerful and general response. It does so because the passages about seeming and being remain constricted to the single topic from a single viewpoint. But chiasmic expressions globally imply that such a focus is not possible. For not only do they repeatedly cross us and exhibit for analysis multiple views and measures of manifold associations, antitheses, and tradeoffs, but they also interweave inextricable domains through myriad substitutions, omissions, and extensions. Indeed, through chiasmus one can trace the history of scholarly scrutiny of impingements long acknowledged to be difficult in *Measure for Measure* (such as integrity/corruption or spiritual wit/physical will of character). And through it as well one can trace those impingements recently brought to attention (such as public manipulation and enforcement of private morality). The predominance of chiasmus in *Measure for Measure* thus seems to support Katharine Eisaman Maus's thesis that the play sets up and maintains simultaneously contradictory claims that human beings and our chief production, societies, are both fundamentally alike and radically different.[14] But since chiasmus follows her primary view of inner versus outer less than her understanding of the play's compulsion of multitudinous interpretations, chiasmus might seem more in line with the hypotheses of Patricia Parker. For the extraordinary proliferation of chiasmic expressions in the play does more than compel our attention to these irresolvable problems in *Measure for Measure*. It also encourages us to predict that chiasmic expressions will draw attention to other irresolvable problems in the play that criticism has yet to interrogate fully. In the final analysis, however, instead of the open-endedness Parker stresses, what chiasmus does in *Measure for Measure* is require us to focus, to stop and ponder the very intractability of problems of justice and mercy, that crucial domain wherein proliferating entailments from other domains are perpetually constructing identities, oppositions, relationships, and exchanges.

The potency of chiasmus, as Peacham suggests, comes from how its confuting and inverting of terms stops us and from how its syntactical display insists that we measure identity and association, opposition and relation. Thus ensuring that we estimate complexities and difficulties more than we judge consequences, this figure helps to configure *Measure for Measure* as a problem play for formal, syntactic reasons as well as for the thematic reason of presenting vexatious links between justice and mercy.

Two goals might follow from this result. In general, it seems reasonable to claim for a working premise that rhetorical schemes may help us understand others among Shakespeare's plays; more generally yet, whenever we think about literary techniques we need to consider the uses of schematic figures just as we consider the uses of tropes and images in enabling, testing, accommodating, and proliferating interpretations. In specific, it seems reasonable to pursue as a working premise that other rhetorical practices might help us earn a sounder grounding for understanding Shakespeare's problem plays and the other interrelated problem plays of the era. More specifically yet, we might try thinking about *All's Well That Ends Well* at least partly in terms of aphorisms and other accompanying devices that challenge and entrap and about *Troilus and Cressida* in terms of the witty, admired styles employed by its three dominant rhetoricians, Pandarus, Ulysses, and Thersites, to influence others.

4

The Trappings of *All's Well That Ends Well*

Just before Bertram enters to exult over what he believes to be a liaison with Diana and to witness his comrades' unmasking of his tutor Paroles as a miles gloriosus, both lords Dumaine are considering news of the death of Helen, his wife and yet no wife:

> SECOND LORD DUMAINE I am heartily sorry that he'll be glad of this.
>
> FIRST LORD DUMAINE How mightily sometimes we make us comforts of our losses.
>
> SECOND LORD DUMAINE And how mightily some other times we drown our gain in tears. The great dignity that his valour hath here acquired for him shall at home be encountered with a shame as ample.
>
> FIRST LORD DUMAINE The web of our life is of a mingled yarn, good and ill together. Our virtues would be proud if our faults whipped them not, and our crimes would despair if they were not cherished by our virtues. (4.3.61–72)[1]

What draws my immediate interest to these lines is not so much the reversals in thought as the reversals in style, what might be called the trappings of the passage.

After an initial expression of disapproval and disappointment in Bertram's response to the death of his wife, there appear a pair of witty, epigrammatic statements marked by phrasal anaphora that is followed by an application in a chiasmus and then an aphorism based on a commonplace image that is then explicated by another chiasmus. The first and second lords' anaphoras point to an abstract inversion (Bertram will take as a personal advantage what is in fact a loss) and its reversed expression of crying over achievements. This is followed by the second lord's specific application to Bertram: the glory that he has won in Florence will be received in France with at least an equivalent shame. Then the first lord completes the set when he uses an emblem to observe that personal life consists of threads of good and evil tangled like yarn before he concludes with a climactic chiasmus about the inseparability of human virtues from the canceling, humiliating failings and immoralities twisted together with them. What is fascinating here is the expression of perpetually balanced antitheses of private human emotions in comfort and loss with their public moral entailments of approval and disapproval over virtues and sins. Moreover, in people these oppositions are always implicated and ever remain inextricable. Slight comfort may be gleaned from "virtues" opening and closing the figure, perhaps thereby suggesting a hopeful outcome.

Thus isolated the two lords' observations appear more abstract than specific. But fellow officers have in mind a direct application to Bertram. And we have in mind a context of language and action already displayed earlier in the scene and earlier throughout *All's Well That Ends Well*. The lords Dumaine have just finished discussing the shame Bertram has already incurred by way of a scolding from his mother and a fall from the favor of his guardian and king. Both result from his failure as a husband who deserted his wondrous wife before consummation of his marriage. Moreover, they have just revealed the even greater shame in husbandry that he is accruing by arranging an adulterous liaison. The emblem of this is his surrender to his prospective prize of the ancient family ring handed down from father to son. In language tinted by the martial terms whereby Bertram has won renown, they have been describing Bertram's equivalent campaign for shame. He will be chastened for making "chastity" "unchaste," for having committed treason against himself, since aphoristically "he that in this action contrives against his own nobility, in his proper stream o'erflows himself" (4.3.23–25). The lords can only hope that when Bertram witnesses the disgraceful betrayals by the talkative Paroles, his ambushed martial tutor, Bertram will scrutinize his own actions, "see his company anatomized, that he might take a measure of his own judgements, wherein so curiously he had set this counterfeit" (4.3.32–34). We extend the two lords' immediate context to include habitual talk through *All's Well* about Bertram's blend of equally potent failings and achievements, about the mingling of sex and love in terms of warfare, in terms of challenging and winning and losing, especially in terms of undermining and blowing up, and most of all in terms of traps and ambushes, the employment of trickery replete with recurring emblems such as rings and vividly aphoristic and enigmatic figurative expressions. The scene thus exhibits how all this talk replicates, often as speech acts, the actions that dominate *All's Well That Ends Well*.

That is, the figurative trappings of the passage that drew my immediate interest inevitably drew me as well to trappings as actions carried out and to trappings as a mode of plotting, in multiple senses. "Trappings" replicates or implicates its own doubled etymology. Coming from Middle English, "trappings" is defined by the *Oxford English Dictionary* as "a cloth or covering spread over the harness or saddle of a horse or other beast of burden, often gaily ornamented." As it derives from the Old English gerund for "adorn," it fits the ancient metaphor for rhetorical figuration, the adornment or clothing of ideas in language, and can refer to their application in writing and analysis. But inasmuch as it follows from the Middle Latin term, "trappa," "trap" or "snare," it can refer as well to the kinds of entrapments people lay for others and authors set to win audiences.[2] Thus in the very term matter and manner are fused in multiple ways. Similarly, I want to claim, matter and manner in *All's Well That Ends Well* are fused in multiple ways.

The two lords' stylistic moment—their trappings of ordered balance and antithesis, reversed chiasmus, figured aphorism, and wit—becomes in other passages of *All's Well* more curt, more gnomic. Because such moments appear extensively throughout the play, they promise another opportunity to consider Shakespeare from the perspective of stylistic figuration, just as we considered the uses of chiasmus as one key to understanding another of Shakespeare's problem plays, *Measure for Measure*. Both belong among the problem plays that dominated the London stage at the end of Elizabeth's reign and the beginning of James's. This means *All's Well* belongs with plays that depend, to a discomforting degree, on trickery and reversals, most often sexual trickery combined with some combination of familial economic and sociopolitical calculation, where characters vie to outwit each other for gain. And it means *All's Well*'s style belongs with these same plays that abound in proverbs, gnomes, terse sayings, puzzles, riddles, and wit contests to express and embody the characters' overly abundant intellectual and emotional challenges, counter-challenges, and entrapments of each other.

There is a long list of other significant critical issues: uneasiness over a folk tale quest and achievement of impossible tasks as a pattern for a woman rather than a man; queasiness over the bed trick she plays on her husband and her manipulativeness; antipathy toward her objective as unworthy of her desire; dissatisfaction with his inadequately motivated concluding conversion; difficulties with the general aggressive sexual mood; preoccupation with contests between experienced counsel and rash youth; communal versus personal choices in life; public needs versus private feelings in sexual mores, and more.[3] Nevertheless, I focus on the multiple trappings of *All's Well That Ends Well.* And I reiterate a neglected thesis suggested by Madeleine Doran about trickery and developed by Phyllis Gorfain in the context of folk riddles: *All's Well That Ends Well* "is a problem in wit, not [I substitute, before it is a problem] in manners or morals."[4] I base my approach as well on the renewed premise that attentiveness to formal considerations renders clues in literary works. Like, say, Gerard Genette, in *Narrative Discourse*, I assume that narration and theme are replicated or formalized in macro as well as in micro devices that we need to describe. And, like Maureen Quilligan in *The Language of Allegory*, I believe in "the generation of narrative structure out of wordplay" (22) or, to reword, in the interactive formulation of narration and figuration. In order to pursue this fundamental theme in *All's Well* among problem plays, I discuss style, then plots and plot, and finally theme.

Trappings in Language

Little wonder that at least for a few plays Shakespeare was tempted to try his hand at a style that proved successful for fellow playwrights. Small surprise that he chose for *All's Well That Ends Well* to play with their stylistic emphasis on offering and testing commonplace saws, challenging through common proverbs and sayings, and puzzling through gnomic riddles.

Possessing considerable impact in a diminishing oral culture and an increasingly literate one, prudential maxims provided pervasive communal guidance.[5] In *Elizabethan Rhetoric* Peter Mack reemphasizes the well-known popularity of moral sentences in the rhetorical education system favored in early modern England. They supplied the first material parsed and conned by grammar school students as exempla of Latin syntax and everyday behavior. Mack lists Culman's *Sententiae pueriles*, the collection generally labeled "Cato," and Erasmus's oft-reprinted *Adagia* as studies that were popular and useful at once; moreover, they supplied grist for memorable testimony later when students would compose familiar letters, narratives, and other writings (32–35). This form of plausible support continued to be collected by college students in commonplace books of pithy wit and wisdom readily available to enhance their conversations, their speeches, and their compositions (104–6). It permeates all modes of discourse from personal communication to parliamentary address to history and homily. Beyond providing the proverbial wisdom of the ages, the moral monition of eternal divinity, and the prudential advice of their time emphasized by Mack, aphorisms offered stimuli for contemplation and analysis of matters public and private. Many of Sir Francis Bacon's *Essays* open and proceed by way of introducing such witty sayings and then testing their adequacy through observations, analyses, modifications that refine thought about their import, their impact, and the situations when they take effect. This modus operandi provides a founding principle for Stanley E. Fish's criticism of such familiar attempts as "Of Simulation and Dissimulation" and "Of Love."[6] Bacon's employment suggests another of the multiple uses noted in "*Aphoristic Style*: The Rhetoric of the Aphorism," wherein Gary Saul Morson provides a provisional taxonomy and a provocative set of aphoristic observations about the generically difficult pithy sayings and writings listed under many heads—the proverbs, maxims, slogans, witticisms, and epigrams that have long provided memorable and effective rhetorical tools.[7] Among many shrewd observations, Morson proposes that beyond epitomizing collective wisdom, aphorisms offer modes of realizing, understanding, and discovering (the premise that seems to underwrite Bacon's procedure). He further proposes that such memorable sayings range in use from riddles, which pose problems that imply answers, and dicta, which offer specific practical conclusions, to aphorisms, which prompt searches into mystery. The important moral is that for every aphorism there is an equal and opposite aphorism because the situations and the categories of usage are perpetually shifting so as to test adequacy and to proffer opportunity. *All's Well That Ends Well* explores the shifting uses of such sayings for summing up communal moral and prudential advice, even more for riddling, and most of all for challenging, testing, and sparring wittily, by characters who employ them as "trappings" in every sense of the word.

All's Well That Ends Well is notable for its characters' employment of aphoristic statements, proverbial wisdom, riddles and gnomic banter that set a context for challenges, counter-challenges, and a variety of verbal tricks—a multitude of trappings of and through language. The royal councillor Lafeu opens the play with aphoristic application of the King's general provision to his new ward Bertram: "He that so generally is at all times good must of necessity hold his virtue to you." Proverbs especially supply pointed wisdom to the conversation of the senior generation, the Countess and the King as well as the councillor. More constrained than Polonius, the Countess still sends Bertram off to court with a string of advisory aphorisms: "Thy blood and virtue / Contend for empire in thee, and thy goodness / Share with thy birthright. Love all, trust a few, / Do wrong to none" (1.1.55ff.). Later she observes in another cluster of aphorisms that Helen's behavior betrays a young woman in love: "If ever we are nature's, these are ours: this thorn / Doth to our rose of youth rightly belong. / Our blood to us, this to our blood is born" (1.3.113ff.). The King offers still another treasure trove of precepts for Bertram in his nostalgic descriptions of Bertram's model father, centered by "So like a courtier, contempt nor bitterness / Were in his pride or sharpness; if they were / His equal had awaked them, and his honour-Clock to itself—knew the true minute when / Exception bid him speak, and at this time/ His tongue obeyed his hand" (1.2.36–41). The King's long, oft-quoted speech about the necessity of merit for earning and maintaining honor seems a consequence of the earlier set of moral maxims: "From lowest place when virtuous things proceed, / The place is dignified by th' doer's deed. / Where great additions swell's and virtue none, / It is a dropsied honour" (2.3.121ff.). Helen's opening use of the aphoristic and enigmatic "I do affect a sorrow indeed, but I have it too" (1.1.47) has with others been annotated since at least Charles and Mary Cowden Clarke's edition of the 1860s. Helen demonstrates wisdom beyond her years in part by her effective employment of proverbs. To cap the first scene, she exhorts herself by way of a string of aphorisms about self-reliance in quest of her seemingly impossible goal, Bertram. "Our remedies oft in ourselves do lie / Which we ascribe to heaven. The fated sky / Gives us free scope, only doth backward pull / Our slow designs when we ourselves are dull" continues in the same mode (1.1.199ff.).

More often the aphoristic style in *All's Well* is employed to puzzle, to tease, and especially to challenge. The master who professes this mode of wit, and calls attention to the fact, is the clown Lavatch. He it is who notes proverbial wisdom's implicit claim to meet every occasion, to provide a "bountiful answer that fits all questions" (2.2.13). Then he it is who is compelled to confess the countering practicalities that arise from different situations: "I see things may serve long, but not serve ever" (2.2.48–49). For it is he who proposes "O Lord, sir!" to be the perfect response to any demand, as appropriate as "the barber's chair that fits all buttocks . . . the nail to his hole, the cuckold to his horn . . . the pudding to his skin" (2.2.14–24), before the Countess rebuts his challenge with her playful threat of a whipping. Lavatch's quick tactical retraction here indicates how he repeatedly maneuvers through the riddling, puzzling, challenging mode. For example, by means of a string of popular proverbial observations he argues that whoever cuckolds him serves as his drudge for doing his chores and as his friend for loving him. These are epitomized in "He that ears my land spares my team" and "he that cherishes my flesh and blood loves my flesh and blood" (1.3.38–39, 41–42). Lavatch sets up as well a pattern of aphoristic satirical commentary: "Though honesty be no puritan, yet it will do no hurt; it will wear the surplice of humility over the black gown of a big heart" (1.3.82– 84). Later at court he employs similar aphoristic paradoxes to explain to Helen how the Duchess can be simultaneously unwell and well, being on earth rather than in heaven (2.4.1–11).

To this puzzling, riddling mode in the foreground, Lavatch adds other related trappings of language that emphasize the central themes of *All's Well*. He confuses waging war with making love when he purportedly comforts the Duchess about Bertram's running away to the battles of Florence: "The danger is in standing to't; that's the loss of men, though it be the getting of children" (3.2.39–40). Toward the end he reminds the audience that Bertram, and all the world, exhibit an inextricable mix of good and evil, warfare and sexual battle, by way of puzzling, riddling aphorisms. These range from announcing himself as "a fool, sir, at a woman's service, and a knave at a man's" to acknowledging the potency of "the Black Prince, sir, alias the prince of darkness, alias the devil" who keeps the "broad gate and the great fire" alongside the little house with the "narrow gate." And they include wondering whether the "goodly patch of velvet" on Bertram's left cheek covers a martial or a syphilitic scar (4.5.20–85).

The person at whom puzzling, aphoristic challenges are most often hurled and by whom they are expertly parried is Helen. Paroles initially challenges Helen, and she rebuts him in the early bout of bawdy wit that used to offend critical sensibilities and now attracts them. This exchange draws to attention as well many significant stylistic patterns, mainly recurring terms and images that extend the aphoristic trappings in *All's Well*. Rather than following Patricia Parker's fascinating interest in the "inflation" and "generation" of the scene,[8] I want to follow out Helen's introduction of the more commonplace battle of the sexes imagery that pervades the play. "You have some stain of soldier in you, let me ask you a question. Man is enemy to virginity: how may we barricado it against him?" initiates imagery she sustains in "assails," "valiant in the defense," and "warlike resistance." Her imagery grapples with Paroles's mode of paradoxical aphoristic challenge: "Virginity being blown down, man will quicklier be blown up. . . . Loss of virginity is rational increase, and there was never virgin got till virginity was first lost" (1.1.106–22). Commentators have long noted that both the paradoxes and the image pattern of this fifty-line contest of wit are so curtly commonplace as to be proverbial. They proffer more challenge than puzzle. Similar sets of challenging paradoxes appear as the penultimate series on virginity as self-destructive narcissism and in the final variations on *carpe diem* to persuade the woman to make profitable use of her virginity. Paroles concludes the series by asking Helen a question that challenges: "Will you anything with it?" (1.1.150–51). "Not my virginity, yet . . ." provides Helen's nigh pregnant response (1.1.152).

Such witty trappings lead from Helen's tentative response through her resolutions about self-reliance just later. They proceed to the endearing aphoristic wit through which the Countess discerns her concealed love. This aphoristic wit the Countess in turn extends so as to encourage her to pursue her desire. Rather than tracing out most recent criticism's valuable inquiry into the theme of incest in these lines,[9] I want to focus on the transparent manner of riddling. Dismayed at the Countess calling herself Helen's mother because her guardian, Helen insists that she can accept the Countess' motherhood only if Bertram can be reserved as her lover, not her brother. The Countess, forewarned by the steward who overheard Helen's love lament, determines to surprise Helen by proclaiming her figurative motherhood. The set climaxes in an aphorism:

What's in "mother"
That you start at it? I say I am your mother,
And put you in the catalogue of those
That were enwombed mine. 'Tis often seen
Adoption strives with nature, and choice breeds
A native slip to us from foreign seeds. (1.3.125–30)

As the Countess repeatedly insists on her motherhood by way of grafting, so Helen vehemently denies it, since "The Count Roussillon cannot be my brother. / I am from humble, he from honoured name" (1.3.139–40); she is a vassal, he her lord. The Countess, working round to casting Helen as her daughter-in-law, presses to confirm the obvious:

> You love my son. Invention is ashamed
> Against the proclamation of thy passion
> To say thou dost not. Therefore tell me true.
> . . . .
> If it be so you have wound a goodly clew. (1.3.157–66)

She thus concludes her extended challenge that Helen confess her love by introducing the recurring image of the entangled thread, knot, fabric of life.

This texture of inextricably inwoven desire and avoidance Helen tangles all the more in a reply that at once evades and affirms:

> Be not offended, for it hurts not him
> That he is loved of me. I follow him not
> By any token of presumptuous suit,
> Nor would I have him till I do deserve him,
> Yet never know how that desert should be.
> I know I love in vain, strive against hope;
> Yet in this captious and untenable sieve
> I still pour in the waters of my love
> And lack not to lose still.
> . . . .
> then give pity
> To her whose state is such that cannot choose
> But lend and give where she is sure to lose,
> That seeks to find not that her search implies,
> But riddle-like lives sweetly where she dies. (1.3.180–201)

Several crucial self-challenges are embedded among others in Helen's statement of certain loss in loving Bertram. First, the distance between her own status and Bertram's seems unbridgeable. Second, she desires only what she can earn by her own merit but foresees no hope of proving it. Third, three proverbial images express the degree of her hopelessness. Helen pours her love into a sieve that cannot collect it but instead lets it pass through to waste; Helen is on a pilgrimage seeking to avoid what she searches for; and Helen's life no less than her riddle fails for lack of expressing itself. Helen thereby earns the Countess's sympathy and support in an attempt to prove her merit by trying to cure the King of his fistula in proof of her merit.

Helen comes armed with proverbial assurances to undertake the challenge of her first impossible folklore task, to cure the King of his apparently terminal malady and so be offered a husband as her prize. But she must rebut a set of witty proverbial challenges by the King to get to attempt his cure. The scene is set by strained jovial riddling between the loyal councillor, who attempts to cheer his sovereign and introduce a new treatment, and the King who, wearied of failed attempts, fobs off hope. Likening the King to the fox that claims grapes it cannot reach (like good health) must be sour, Lafeu tries to cajole the King into interest in "Doctor She's" cure. Because the King can reasonably "esteem / A senseless help, when help past sense we deem" (2.1.121–22), Helen challenges his rationality by appealing to faith in the familiar Christian paradox that God employs the lowliest means to accomplish the greatest tasks. Her series of riming maxims affirming the miraculous includes:

> He that of greatest works is finisher
> Oft does them by the weakest minister.
> So holy writ in babes hath judgement shown
> When judges have been babes. . . .
> . . . .
> Oft expectation fails, and most oft there
> Where most it promises, and oft it hits
> Where hope is coldest and despair most fits.
> . . . .
> But know I think, and think I know most sure,
> My art is not past power, nor you past cure. (2.1.134–57)

Helen persists in witty exhortation that she will serve only as God's curative agent until the King finally submits: "Methinks in thee some blessed spirit doth speak, / His powerful sound within an organ weak." So he makes a contract challenging her with the ultimate penalty for failure and offering her greatest desire for success. If she fails she sentences herself to death, but if she succeeds "Then shalt thou give me with thy kingly hand / What husband in thy power I will command" (2.1.174–75, 192–93).

Helen's wondrous, folkloristic achievement of the first impossible task of curing the King brings on a second, even greater challenge. By the time Bertram offers this challenge to his wife, the context of riddling challenges in general and to Helen in specific has already been firmly established by encounters with Paroles, the Countess, and the King. The harshness of Bertram's challenge is aggravated by the insult and injury of being denied two of the principal choices generally available to youth, spouse and profession. The bridegroom chafes as his peers leave him behind at court while they become condottieri winning spurs in Italy (2.1.1–58).[10] From the moment the King assigns him to marry Helen, he protests in public, "But follows it, my lord, to bring me down / Must answer for your raising?" and he vows in private, "they have married me. / I'll to the Tuscan wars and never bed her" (2.3.108–9, 256–57). Both Bertram's pent fury and the play's riddling and challenging mode are crucial to understanding Bertram's challenge to Helen by the traditional mode of transparent riddles in letters.[11] In that to his mother he repeats in abrupt antonym, rime, and pun his previously private asseverations refusing any more than a ceremonial marriage: "I have sent you a daughter-in-law. She hath recovered the King and undone me. I have wedded her, not bedded her, and sworn to make the 'not' eternal" (3.2.19–21). To his wife he sends a distressing dismissal and a seemingly impossible challenge. Reading, Helen shudders: "here's my passport. 'When thou canst get the ring upon my finger, which never shall come off, and show me a child begotten of thy body that I am father to, then call me husband; but in such a "then" I write a "never."' This is a dreadful sentence. . . . 'Till I have no wife, I have nothing in France.' 'Tis bitter" (3.2.54–73). As Helen begins her pilgrimage abroad in hopes that Bertram will then avoid the dangers of war, Bertram completes the challenge in laying claim to the combat of men instead of the battle of the sexes. He pledges to the Duke of Florence that "I shall prove / A lover of thy drum, hater of love" (3.3.10–11). The instrument that pounds out the alarms of war drowns out Helen's sexuality as it re-echoes through the next scenes.

Bertram's challenge to Helen is recalled by other challenges until she reveals her victory. It is recalled as well by more trappings of language begun in Helen's first encounter with Paroles and continued through *All's Well*'s middle scenes. The conflation of battle of the sexes with achieving manhood in warfare language appears intermittently. The King, for instance, exhorts the departing young lords to seek out the fame of warfare but to "Beware of being captives [of "Those girls of Italy"] / Before you serve" (2.1.10–22). It appears as well when Lafeu persists in offering challenging, multiple punning insults to Paroles, now servant to his master's new mistress. He has "found" Paroles to be a miles gloriosus, counterfeit traveler, exercise dummy: "when I lose thee again I care not. Yet art thou good for nothing but taking up" (2.3.199–200). Paroles's cowardice appears through his martial language and apparel as well as his evasions of Lafeu's challenge. Bertram, who continually follows Paroles's advice, also ignores Lafeu's challenges that Paroles is a clown who has "made shift to run into't, boots and spurs and all, like him that leaped into the custard" (2.5.34–35ff).

In Tuscany the lords Dumaine take up Lafeu's challenges of Paroles. They warn Bertram against the fraudulent mentor, propose to try him by ambush, and urge Bertram to bear witness to his betrayal of comrades and then punish him by giving him the proverbial "John Drum's entertainment" for falsely laying claim to a daring recapture of a drum humiliatingly lost to the enemy (3.6.34). To carry out the challenge these lords also take up the other trappings of language, entrapping Paroles by employing nonsensical words to confuse and confute the man named after words. They thereby convict and punish for loving words "No more than a fish loves water" the man who claims to "love not many words" (3.6.75–76). The bushwhackers "speak what terrible language [they] will. Though you understand it not yourselves, no matter, for we must not seem to understand him, unless some one among us, whom we must produce for an interpreter" (4.1.2–5). So all use "linsey-woolsey," "choughs' language, gabble enough" except for the "very politic interpreter" (4.1.10, 18–19), whom Paroles implores to communicate with him in any Germanic or Romantic tongue so that he can reveal his comrades' secrets.

Particularly pertinent to the riddling, challenging trappings of language are the poem Paroles has written to warn the Florentine maiden against Bertram's treacherous pursuit, the punning of the captors as they seem on the verge of executing him, and his comments after he learns that he has been duped. The doggerel verse unmasks the treachery of Bertram's "devoted friend, sir, the manifold linguist and the armipotent soldier" (4.3.223–24). By way of a series of punning challenges it accuses Bertram of reneging on debts, "scores," warns against his "matches," casts doubt on his manhood and sexuality, and "counts" him a fool (4.3.223–24, 212–18). Then the interpreter honors his butt Paroles's request to "let me see my death" by agreeing "That shall you, and take your leave of all your friends" as he removes the blindfold to let Paroles see the comrades he has betrayed (4.3.287–88). Releasing Paroles, the interpreter continues to pun, suggests the tangled skein motif, and recalls Bertram's punning challenge of the marriage: "You are undone, captain—all but your scarf; that has a knot on't yet" (4.3.300–301). Finally Paroles sums up the scene with an admonitory maxim, a vow to persevere, and a pair of exhortative rimed proverbs: "Who knows himself a braggart, / Let him fear this, for it will come to pass / That every braggart shall be found an ass. / Rust, sword; cool, blushes, and Paroles live / Safest in shame; being fooled, by fool'ry thrive. / There's place and means for every man alive."

Meanwhile Helen and her supporters answer Bertram's challenge in the same linguistic trappings, imagery from the battle of the sexes and the honor won by men, she helped Paroles initiate during their early bawdy encounter. Hints appear in her epistolary sonnet informing the Countess about taking a pilgrimage so as to allow Bertram to return "home in peace" from "the bloody course [including curse] of war" where "death and danger dogs the heels of worth" (3.4.10, 8, 15).[12] Again she alludes to the martial love complex when she describes Bertram "Lay[ing] down his wanton siege before [Diana's] beauty, / Resolved to carry her" and proposes that in response Diana "seems as won . . . appoints him an encounter . . . delivers me to fill the time" (3.7.18–19, 31–33). Helen's seconds sustain the same figurative terms. A friend of Diana's mother warns that Paroles is "a filthy officer" and that Bertram's "promises, enticements, oaths, tokens, and all their engines of lust are not the things they go under," while the widow avows that her daughter is "armed for [Bertram], and keeps her guard / In honestest defense" (3.5.15–18, 69–71). Diana proves suggestive in the very scene when she seems hard won to succumb to Bertram's strategy: she first challenges that honor champions her "part / Against [his] vain assault" but then surrenders to his victory when he has "conquered my yet maiden bed" (4.2.51–52, 65–66). Diana's aphoristic rumination concludes the scene: "in this disguise I think't no sin / To cozen him that would unjustly win." This capping couplet acknowledges that the challenging trappings of language work in concert with, indeed are enabled to work because they also signify an array of traps laid by characters for each other. Linked are the trappings, often labeled false endings, laid by Shakespeare throughout *All's Well That Ends Well.*

Trappings in Action

Causing more of Harbage's moral qualms and drawing more strictures than the knotty/naughty language are the actions of characters in problem comedies that include *All's Well That Ends Well.* The staple plots of problem comedies consist of the intrigues and manipulations of some shrewd politico outwitting tricky competitors in pursuit of economic and sociopolitical success. Prominent scenarios include the dubiously virtuous Machiavellian machinations of an exiled ruler who strives to regain his kingdom and family despite a usurping politician's counter-ploys (*The Malcontent* and its offspring *The Fleer*); the scams of smart, ambitious young men of no status who form ventures to defraud gulls (*The Alchemist*); the cynical Italianate finaglings and bold assaults of a bankrupt younger son on a dual quest to gain wealth and status by way of marriage to a well-placed and -endowed widow and also to supplant his timid elder as head of an ancient house (*The Widow's Tears*); and most generally, the connivings of some gallant against a father, a brother, an uncle, a patron, a usurer, a power broker in hot pursuit of a wealthy widow or an heiress. Perhaps stereotypical is the plot that involves the bankrupt young gallant who tricks a shrewd, manipulative usurer into pursuing and marrying his castoff whore disguised as an heiress, or into mistaking as achievement the appearance that the gallant has gone through with a widow, so that after numerous ploys and counter-ploys, twists and surprises and revelations he regains his reputation and wherewithal. Such is the basic plot employed from Thomas Middleton's seminal *A Trick to Catch the Old One* (1604) to Philip Massinger's satiric *A New Way to Pay Old Debts* (1625). Through such scenarios a gallant gains victory and displays manhood above the pack by means of his wit, that is, his clever sexual, social, economic manipulations. *All's Well* makes a woman its victor in this battle of wits. And since Helen is sponsored by a monarch, her aspirations can aim higher than most of her male counterparts.

The trappings of various characters throughout *All's Well That Ends Well* have already made their appearances, but they deserve to be highlighted, along with their linguistic trappings that expand on the challenging and entrapping employment of aphoristic language. Early on, while puzzles unravel slowly, traps are sparse. Then, beginning with Bertram's challenge to Helen they become dense. Not insignificantly, this series of traps is set with the pun on "not" as negation and "knot" as emblem of marriage. Bertram challenges "I have wedded her, not bedded her, and sworn to make the 'not' eternal" (3.2.20–21). The "not" continues to resonate in the "never" of Helen's opportunity to gain his family ring and bear his child and the sexual punning of "nothing" in its reiterated burden, "Till I have no wife, I have nothing in France" (3.2.58, 72).

The dominant central traps are those that the lords Dumaine lay for Paroles and that Helen lays for Bertram—the former in reaction to Paroles's braggadocio, the latter in response to Bertram's challenge. Each entrapment is signaled by a property, an instrumental emblem of one trap that serves as well as a reminder of the other—the drum and the ring. Their association is linked from Bertram's earlier choice of the drum of Florence's warfare rather than love, "I shall prove / A lover of thy drum, hater of love" (3.3.10–11). He makes an apparently unwitting pun on the sexual referent for "drum" that is identical to that of "ring" here and in *The Merchant of Venice* and to that in the con artist Face's pounding reiteration to the whore Dol Common, "thy drum, / Thy drum, Dol, thy drum" in Jonson's *The Alchemist* (3.3.44–45). And it is frequently repeated, as in a casual conjunction when Paroles frets about the troops' loss of a drum while Mariana scorns him as the "ring-carrier" from Bertram to Diana (3.5.87, 90).

The drum that sounds a marching or attacking rhythm provides emblem and motif for the entrapment of Paroles. Paroles returns to Florence from a skirmish so visibly "vexed" about the loss of one drum (3.5.87–88) that he continues to thump away at this challenge until to save face he is obliged to try to recapture another. The lords Dumaine take advantage of the braggart's reiterated "stratagem" to "fetch his drum" so as to lay their entrapping ambush. When he betrays all, they reward him with "Jack Drum's entertainment." Even Bertram late, like Lafew early, "shall find him" (3.6.31, 34, 94). Preparing for action, Paroles brags of tactics and self-exhortations: "I will presently pen down my dilemmas, encourage myself in my certainty, put myself into my mortal preparation; and by midnight look to hear further from me" (3.6.65–68).[13] But he approaches the ambush scared of the predicament his "too foolhardy" tongue has led him into; imagines how, like Falstaff, he might cover his cowardice by wounding himself superficially; and wishes he might find a drum. Waylaid and fearing death for lack of a common tongue, he volunteers, "I'll discover that which shall undo the Florentine" (4.1.67). Under interrogation he insults as he betrays his fellows until they reveal their trap. In humiliation he laments: "I'll no more drumming. A plague of all drums" (4.3.278).

Equally obvious and reiterated ring references provide the emblem and motif for Helen's entrapment of Bertram. Yet her very entrapment of him, as its emblem, is made possible by Bertram's own second attempt at entrapment, the seduction of Diana. Diana's advisors all note the nature of the entrapment, the "enticements," "engines of lust," decoys, springs, "limed twigs" that Bertram employs with his "ring-bearer" Paroles to catch her (3.5.17, 18, 22). He himself alludes to them when talking to the first lord Dumaine (3.6.99–107).

As the women reiterate, Helen merely takes advantage of Bertram's attempt to trap Diana in order to trap him. Though the Widow, Diana's mother, does not immediately understand, she quickly catches on to the bed trick and to the importance of the ring as the heirloom of the patriarchal family, while Helen is outlining the stratagem to entrap Bertram through Diana seeming to fall for his trap:

> You see it lawful then. It is no more
> But that your daughter ere she seems as won
> Desires this ring; appoints him an encounter;
> In fine, delivers me to fill the time,
> Herself most chastely absent. (3.7.31–35)

In the aphoristic, gnomic style involving rime, parallel oppositions, and chiasmus that characterizes *All's Well,* Helen sums up the biter-bit morality of Bertrand's entrapment. Moreover, the entrapment offers the advantage of a sexual congress in lawful marriage rather than in adulterous liaison. Helen's good intent will invert and surpass Bertram's ill one:

> Let us essay our plot, which if it speed
> Is wicked meaning in a lawful deed
> And lawful meaning in a wicked act,
> Where both not sin, and yet a sinful fact.

The entrapment of Bertram is carried out by Diana on stage since Helen's bed trick is not presented. It accentuates the importance and the morality of trapping. After the initial skirmish wherein Bertram swears service and Diana suspects false oaths, she requires a test of his sexual fidelity: "Give me that ring" (4.2.40). The value of the ring as emblem of the generational family jewels, Bertram's masculine family heritage and loyalty, the "honour" of "his house," is counterpoised by the value of Diana's "honour" for "her house," her family's generational jewel, feminine family heritage and loyalty through unmarried virginity and marital fidelity. This heavily laden passage forms the burden of the familiar exchange until Bertram gives Diana his family ring, falls for Helen's trap. Making graphic the sexuality of the trade through the image of a wedding ring on a finger, Diana lets Bertram know other conditions of darkness, silence, and brevity in bed that make up still more of Helen's trap in the exchange of marriage for liaison, herself for Diana:

> And on your finger in the night I'll put
> Another ring that, what in time proceeds,
> May token to the future our past deeds.

Framing these multiply referenced, deeply sexual lines, come their enigmatic, duplicitous entry and ending that predict the final revelation fulfilling Helen's trap for Bertrand:

> My reasons are most strong, and you shall know them
> When back again this ring shall be delivered—
> . . . .
> Adieu till then; then, fail not. You have won
> A wife of me, though there my hope be done. (4.2.60–66)

In departure Bertram gathers that his trap has worked, whereas Diana lets him know, again as a riddle and a challenge, that he has achieved more than he realizes in being trapped himself:

> BERTRAM A heaven on earth I have won by wooing thee.
>
> DIANA For which live long to thank both heaven and me.
> You may so in the end.

Alone, Diana considers the morality of Bertram's seduction trick, his promise of marriage on his wife's death, and of Helen's bed and marital trick. Then she draws her conclusion at the scene's conclusion:

> Since Frenchmen are so braid
> Marry that will; I live and die a maid.
> Only, in this disguise I think't no sin
> To cozen him that would unjustly win.[14]

The two central entrapments come together in the early moments of the scene that completes the trapping of Paroles. There the trappings in the dialogue of the lords Dumaine that opened my inquiry explicitly entwine the entrapment of Paroles with Bertram's anticipated entrapment of Diana. Both man and count are found guilty and in need of chastisement. Each will serve as "the whip of the other" (4.3.36). Bertram enters flushed with his evening's accomplishments. He has bade farewell to the past in Florence (warfare, duke, and city) as well as to his wife, and he salutes the future in his return home to his mother. He is headier still in anticipation of two more immediate events: he has "affected many nicer needs. The last was the greatest, but that I have not ended yet. . . . But shall we have this dialogue between the Fool and the Soldier? Come, bring forth this counterfeit model" (4.3.88–95). We have just learned, of course, that his exultation over the entrapment of Diana is to be replaced by humiliation over his own entrapment, akin to that of Paroles. Far more than Paroles's, however, Bertram's entrapment finally saves as it condemns.

But this moment interweaving the entrapments merely knots the skein that has been entangled through the alternating entrapments of the central portion of *All's Well That Ends Well.* All along scenes of the lords Dumaine's entrapment of Paroles have alternated with scenes of Bertram's attempted entrapment of Diana and through Diana, Helen's entrapment of him. In act 3, scene 5 Helen learns of Bertram's trap for Diana and so begins planning hers of him; then in scene 6 the lords Dumaine plan the ambush and interrogation of Paroles before Bertram momentarily anticipates his actions. In act 3, scene 7 Helen presents her plan to Diana's mother; then immediately act 4, scene 1 features the ambush of Paroles. Scene 2 shows Bertram laying the bait supposed to entrap Diana but instead taking the bait himself; then scene 3 offers the climactic interrogation and reveals the entrapment of Paroles. Immediately after this series Helen's bed trick of Bertram is omitted. Her revelations appear only in prospect.

Likewise sets of oft-discussed potential endings are interlocked with the linking of the plots. Scholars have long been concerned over the many merely temporary, provisional, or false, endings, the hesitations that mark *All's Well That Ends Well.*[15] Hesitations that could momentarily be considered conclusions essentially review the trappings we have been considering. They evidence Shakespeare's exploitation of the repeated surprises, revelations, and reversals that characterize the domesticated "Italianate intrigue comedy" commonly embedded in problem plays, among which *All's Well* vies for distinction.

Trappings in Conclusion

After the entrapment and unmasking of Paroles offer insight into the vices that are entangled with Bertram's virtues, *All's Well That Ends Well* presents several scenes that anticipate yet postpone the climactic entrapment and revelation of Bertram's skein. Similarly to the former scenes, these concluding scenes have stirred critics to belabor contradictory responses. Ever reiterating the conclusion promised by its title, the play entwines two kinds of scenes: those in which Helen, Diana, and her mother make their way back to the King, seeking yet failing to find him until they finally catch him at Roussillon; and those at Roussillon where the Dowager Countess with the clown Lavatch and the councillor Lafeu mourn reports of Helen's death, await the arrivals of Bertram and the King, and receive the suppliant Paroles. As the characters wend their ways home, so too do major themes wind their ways back, summarizing trappings past and anticipating the final revelation of Bertram's entrapment.

As in the dark comedies by Shakespeare's peers, a witty, enigmatic, proverbial and imagistic style pervades, accentuating the clever challenge and trickery that dominate *All's Well.* Less conspicuous in this modulation into the conclusion is the martial imagery of the drum. Lafeu teases Paroles by identifying him with the drum, once in recognition despite beggar's rags, "How does your drum?" (5.2.35), and twice in the final scene, "He's a good drum, my lord, but a naughty orator" and "Good Tom Drum . . . I'll make sport with thee" (5.2.253, 319–20). The first reference, echoing the pair's first meeting ("O my good lord, you were the first that found me." "Was I, in sooth? And I was the first that lost thee" [5.2.36–37]), and the last recall the prevalent theme of challenge and entrapment. The martial drum and beating, along with the battle of the sexes imagery, give way to the ring and marital trappings. The middle drum reference suggests another prevalent identification, that of Bertram with Paroles, as self-entrapping liars. The identification is introduced just earlier in the scene in the "metaphor" and "simile" of Paroles and Lavatch. Paroles has been "cruelly scratched" by the cat Fortune, an echo of Bertram's identification of Paroles with a despicable cat, "I could endure anything before but a cat, and now he's a cat to me" (5.2.10–27; 4.3.225–26). The marital trapping of Bertram, which prominently features the ring, is set at the opening of the first transition scene in the return to France, when

Helen tells the Widow and Diana of the need to attend the King of France and to rely on his gratitude and recognition (4.4.opening).

Even more this scene maintains the familiar motiv that comes to dominate the gnomic, proverbial language and action of *All's Well*'s conclusion. Helen contemplates the situation through a web of gnomic language that fuses oppositions and makes way for biblical and then commonplace proverbs. Her meditation focuses on the interweaving of good and ill in human affairs, and our mistaking of good for ill and ill for good. Her aim specifies Bertram and his entrapment by her, abetted by his belief that he has trapped Diana. She affirms that the end of the tangle will knot in good fortune, fulfilling her marriage and the play's name:

> O, strange men,
> That can such sweet use make of what they hate,
> When saucy trusting of the cozened thoughts
> Defiles the pitchy night; so lust doth play
> With what it loathes, for that which is away.
> . . . .
> But with that word [yet] the time will bring on summer,
> When briers shall have leaves as well as thorns
> And be as sweet as sharp. . . .
> All's well that ends well; still the fine's the crown.
> Whate'er the course, the end is the renown. (4.4.21–36)

Related imagery continues in the next scene. In opening Lafeu considers the misleading clothing, the fashions and fashioning of Paroles. And in conclusion Lavatch questions the meaning of the "patch of velvet on [Bertram's] face . . . a goodly patch of velvet" that could signify a wound of honor or a sexually transmitted disease. The inextricable tangle of good and ill continues in the disappointment of Helen's party over missing the King but her affirmation of the promise of the play's title (5.1). And it continues in the challenging yet finally forgiving interchange when Lafeu responds to Paroles's petition for mercy after having been turned out: "Out upon thee, knave! Dost thou put upon me at once both the office of God and the devil? One brings thee in grace, and the other brings thee out" (5.2.40–42).

For the climactic scene of *All's Well That Ends Well* all come round to Roussillon to simultaneously enact and bear witness to the humiliating interrogation that reveals Bertram's failings and Helen's plan, the finale of the trap Helen has set and Shakespeare has designed to balance the lords Dumaine's shaming of Paroles.[16] Replicating a scenario that surprises characters by gradually revealing to them what we already know, a scenario Shakespeare repeatedly features and prepares for in the Paroles scene, this one too can be severed into discrete units. A process of turn-revelation-and-stage-reaction dissects Bertram's shame and reprieve. The opening lines down to the King's summary "Be this sweet Helen's knell, and now forget her" (5.3.68) linger over expressions of regret by all, particularly by Bertram, over the "loss" of Helen. They also interweave the theme of the tangle of good and ill before belated realization of someone's value. What seems to constitute proverbial nostalgia rendered in couplets during the King's burial of the past in order to promise the future turns out to adumbrate the gain of that promise by the recovery of the past:

> Our rash faults
> Make trivial price of serious things we have,
> Not knowing them until we know their grave.
> Oft our displeasures, to ourselves unjust,
> Destroy our friends and after weep their dust.
> Our own love waking cries to see what's done,
> While shameful hate sleeps out the afternoon. (5.3.61–67)

The next section, which initially seems a prologue to a new marriage for Bertram, to Lafeu's daughter, instead introduces problems with the ring that Bertram is wearing. Bertram offers Lafeu's daughter the ring placed on his finger, he believes, as a nuptial pledge by Diana. But both Lafeu and the King recognize the ring and its significance as the royal pledge to protect Helen. Bertram mistakenly declares that this identification is wrong, but he knowingly lies that the ring is a token offered by some unnamed Florentine noblewoman he rejected. Meanwhile the King insists on his own identification and challenges Bertram to confess how he got the ring from Helen. For she would willingly have given it up only to her husband in bed or to the King in case of her dire need. Vexations increase until in a fury the King has Bertram taken away and Bertram issues a challenge that turns out to be an unwitting prophecy that answers an enigma:

> If you shall prove
> This ring was ever hers, you shall as easy

Prove that I husbanded her bed in Florence,
Where yet she never was. (5.3.125–28)

The following movement enters with the gentleman who bears a letter from Diana petitioning enforcement of Bertram's promise to marry her and concludes with the appearance of Paroles as a witness on Diana's behalf (5.3.233). This section features Diana's increasingly insistent, often parallel and heaped up, heavily connotative assertions of Bertram's pledge to her:

If you shall marry
You give away this hand, and that is mine;
You give away heaven's vows, and those are mine;
You give away myself, which is known mine,
For I by vow am so embodied yours
That she which marries you must marry me,
Either both or none. (5.3.170–76)

In contrast are Bertram's increasingly desperate, transparent attempts to lie that Diana is "a common gamester to the camp" or an "inf'nite cunning" courtesan or a lady "angl[ing]" to catch him (5.3.190, 218, 214). The first is a palpable lie beyond an evasive attack on reputation, since Diana displays his family ring, "whose high respect and rich validity / Did lack a parallel; yet for all that / He gave it to a commoner o'th'camp, / If I be one" (5.3.194–97). Further phony excuses elicit a call for Paroles as witness. Lafeu's reiterated asseverations of withdrawal from his daughter's engagement to Bertram and the Countess's attentiveness to Bertram's embarrassment highlight the loss of any possible credibility left him. Finally Bertram "boggles" in confessing that the ring identified by the King was Diana's—just as Paroles enters.

This movement begins by public association of the two liars, Bertram and his mentor. It was forecast just earlier in Bertram's complaint to forestall Paroles's testimony: Paroles is "quoted for a most perfidious slave / With all the spots o'th' world taxed and debauched, / Whose nature sickens but to speak a truth . . . That will speak anything" (5.3.207–11). The go-between Paroles indicts Bertram in his very claim not to indict the "honorable gentleman" who has "tricks": in "mad" lust after Diana he "loved her, sir, and loved her not" (5.3.243–44, 249). "Thou art a knave and no knave. . . . an equivocal companion" the King accuses Paroles, the model Bertram has imitated thus far. But the second turn of this penultimate movement in the final scene comes in the King's increasing frustration as he augments his threats so as to learn how Bertram got the ring he gave to Helen. For now Diana blatantly denies some of her previous assertions and equivocates about others. She concludes with a set of riddling entanglements of good and ill in response to the King's query, "Wherefore hast thou accused him all this while?":

> Because he's guilty, and he is not guilty.
> He knows I am no maid, and he'll swear to't;
> I'll swear I am a maid, and he knows not.
> Great King, I am no strumpet; by my life,
> I am either maid or else this old man's [Lafeu's] wife. (5.3.284–90)

There has been no genuine "abuse" of the court's ears. Instead, what has been laid out is a set of further enigmatic aphorisms, riddles. These trappings anatomize Bertram's failed challenge and self-damning trap, and these trappings reveal Helen's successful response and saving trap.

The entangled questions of good and ill, loss and recovery, actions supposed and actual, and the trappings of Bertram all get resolved in the final section. It begins as Diana pronounces the set of enigmatic aphorisms that sum up and explain the bed trick riddles by identifying and introducing Helen:

> Though yet [Bertram] never harmed me, here I quit him.
> He knows himself my bed he hath defiled,
> And at that time he got his wife with child.
> Dead though she be she feels her young one kick.
> So there's my riddle, one that's dead is quick.
> And now behold the meaning. (5.3.296–301)

But Helen, however recognized by the court, remains a "shadow" yet no "shadow," "the name and not the thing" (5.3.303–04) without Bertram's acknowledgment of her as wife. Thus he supplies a new response, "Both, both" of claiming her, begging her "pardon," and pledging to "love her dearly ever ever dearly" (5.3.305, 313). So he too recognizes his wife, now "doubly won." Thereby, explains Gorfain, he confesses for all the characters a recognition that Diana's revelatory riddle is kin to the ultimate stakes, nigh impossibly challenging riddle a condemned man can pose to his judge in order to save himself. Helen has repeatedly posed and risked to save herself and Bertram in their marriage a kind of "neck riddle" (272–73, 275). Proverbs that transmit a culture's wisdom and prudence, witticisms that challenge, manipulate, and entrap, aphorisms that explore—all get woven into riddles that reiterate *All's Well That Ends Well.*

Bertram may or may not have been converted from prodigal to husband, may or may not be worthy. The older generation may rightly or wrongly have compelled the younger. The public interest in private sexual matters may or may not have appropriate extensions or limitations. The coupling of aggression with sexuality may or may not be attractive or repellant, may or may not have appropriate extensions or limitations based on considerations of harm, pleasure, gender, kinship. Whatever resolutions or irresolutions may be proffered, all depend on the simple fact that *All's Well That Ends Well* has declared itself to be one of Shakespeare's contributions to the company of difficult problem plays that dominated the era. They present challenges and counterchallenges, tricks and countertricks, perplexing and disturbing entanglements of good and evil, loss and victory; and they do so by means of riddling and punning, challenging and manipulating proverbial expressions and entangling image patterns that replicate and urge problems that mark the transition from Elizabethan to Jacobean.

Specifically, *All's Well* signals its problems by framing and formulating and focusing them as trappings in every sense set for and overcome by, as well as set and sprung by Helen. Moreover, and more generally, to get at those problems above all requires grappling with their figurations, their trappings small and great, throughout *All's Well That Ends Well,* and beyond. So the King responds appropriately by summing up traditional aphoristic wisdom that ever precariously balances oppositions, that ever hedges for the situation with "yet seems" and "if it end so meet," that ever reserves and questions, that ever concludes and yet denies closure: "All yet seems well; and if it end so meet, / The bitter past, more welcome is the sweet."

5

The Wit of Reflexivity in Shakespeare's *Troilus and Cressida*

In the midst of Shakespeare's *Troilus and Cressida*, Ulysses stages a scene during which each of the Greek leaders passes by Achilles' tent. They pointedly ignore the hero they had heretofore implored to return to combat, thereby employing reverse psychology so that he might resume fighting and they might at long last prevail in their siege of Troy. Finally the shrewd director himself appears before Achilles:

A strange fellow here
Writes me that man, how dearly ever parted,
How much in having, or without or in,
Cannot make boast to have that which he hath,
Nor feels not what he owes, but by reflection–
As when his virtues shining upon others
Heat them, and they retort that heat again
To the first givers.

ACHILLES This is not strange, Ulysses:
The beauty that is borne here in the face
The bearer knows not, but commends itself
To others' eyes; nor doth the eye itself,
That most pure spirit of sense, behold itself,
Not going from itself; but eye to eye opposed,
Salutes each other with each other's form,
For speculation turns not to itself
Till it hath travelled and is mirrored there
Where it may see itself. This is not strange at all.

ULYSSES I do not strain at the position—
It is familiar—but at the author's drift,
Who in his circumstance expressly proves
That no man is the lord of anything,
Though in and of him there be much consisting,
Till he communicate his parts to others;
Nor doth he of himself know them for aught
Till he behold them formed in the applause
Where they're extended, who like an arch reverb'rate
The voice again, or like a gate of steel
Fronting the sun, receives and renders back
His figure and his heat. I was rapt in this,
And apprehended here immediately
The unknown Ajax. (3.3.95–125)[1]

As Achilles and Ulysses point out, the notion of reflexivity—our realization of some notion about ourselves when and only when we believe that others recognize and confirm our sense of it—is a time-honored commonplace. The notion can be regarded as a profound ideal emanating from a Platonic dialogue; as a physical observation often called "looking babies" in someone's eyes; as a popular Renaissance conception of sight whereby the eye transmits beams that capture and retrieve some object; or as a stimulating psychological and sociological rediscovery of the twentieth century. Also commonplace is Ulysses' use of this commonplace to move Achilles to acknowledge, at least unconsciously, his double, Ajax, a miles gloriosus who reflects Achilles' vanity. It is precisely this commonplace and its shrewd political employment that offers foundation for a rhetorical consideration of Shakespeare's play. For if *Troilus and Cressida* demonstrates anything, it demonstrates the necessity of reflexivity in wit, a demand that one's own cleverness be ostentatiously recognized and approved, applauded by some audience.

Memorial recognition in audiences through history constitutes the most enduring if not the most compelling form of the reflexivity of wit. Shakespeare counts on it for identification, for naming, when he establishes a refrain based on three names. Just prior to this scene featuring Ulysses and Achilles on reflexivity, to confirm the consummation devoutly wished by Troilus and Cressida and negotiated by Pandarus the three swear the infamous oaths by their names that echo through the play and through literary, and lexicographical, history:

> TROILUS True swains in love shall in the world to come
> Approve their truth by Troilus. . . .
> . . . .
> Yet after all comparisons of truth,
> As truth's authentic author to be cited,
> 'As true as Troilus' shall crown up the verse
> And sanctify the numbers.
>
> CRESSIDA Prophet may you be!
> If I be false, or swerve a hair from truth,
> When time is old and hath forgot itself,
> . . . .
> yet let memory
> From false to false among false maids in love,
> Upbraid my falsehood: when they've said 'as false as
> . . . .
> Yea, let them say to stick the heart of falsehood,
> 'As false as Cressid.'
>
> PANDARUS Go to, a bargain made: seal it, seal it, I'll be the witness. Here I hold your hand, here my cousin's. If ever you prove false one to another, since I have taken such pains to bring you together, let all pitiful goers-between be called to the world's end after my name: call them all panders; let all constant men be Troiluses, all false women Cressids, and all brokers-between panders. Say Amen. (3.2.153–82)

The names and their subsequent significations resound throughout the play. They echo in Cressida's recall when advised that she is to be restored to her father among the Greeks and so has to leave Troilus: "O you gods divine, / Make Cressid's name the very crown of falsehood / If ever she leave Troilus!" (4.2.96–98). They echo again in Troilus's redefinition of his own qualities as she departs: "Whiles others fish with craft for great opinion, / I with great truth catch mere simplicity. . . . Fear not my truth. The moral of my wit / Is 'plain and true': there's all the reach of it" (4.4.102–07). Above all they reverberate in Pandarus's witty doggerel that serves as epilogue to the play after the fall of Hector and Troy. Dismissed by Troilus, "Hence broker-lackey!

Ignomy and shame / Pursue thy life, and live aye with thy name," he intones a mock lament:

> A goodly medicine for my aching bones. O world, world—thus is the poor agent despised. O traitors and bawds, how earnestly are you set a-work, and how ill requited!
> Why should our endeavour be so loved and the performance so loathed? What verse for it? . . . Good traders in the flesh, set this in your painted cloths:
> As many as be here of panders' hall,
> Your eyes, half out, weep out at Pandar's fall.
> Or if you cannot weep, yet give some groans,
> Though not for me yet for your aching bones.
> Brethren and sisters of the hold-door trade,
> Some two months hence my will shall here be made.
> It should be now, but that my fear is this:
> Some galled goose of Winchester would hiss.
> Till then I'll sweat and seek about for eases,
> And at that time bequeath you my diseases.

So, punning multiply, wittily, and scurrilously on pimping (now pandering), on whoring, on venereal diseases, their environs, penalties, and cures as swine on spits, Pandarus sums up a dominant perspective on Troilus, Cressida, and himself. They supply names that for posterity connote, signify, certify, personify fidelity, exigent infidelity, and sexual and social brokerage.

Proclaiming Wit, Rhetoric, Dark Comedy

A perspective of witty display is precisely what "A Never Writer to an Ever Reader" heralds in a reissue of the play, also in 1609, newly entitled *The Famous Historie of Troylus and Cresseid. Excellently expressing the beginning of their loues, with the conceited wooing of Pandarus Prince of Licia. Written by William Shakespeare*. This reissue, instead of advertising a performance by the King's Men at the Globe, promotes interest in the couple's love and especially calls to attention the conceits, the ingenious witty concepts and rhetorical display of a character newly nominated to prominence, Pandarus. Naming these three memorable personages and specifying a tone constitute two among several significant changes in focus that give rise to further speculations about *Troilus and Cressida*. Another comes when the "Never Writer"'s blurb heralds a new genre for the play. It is, he proclaims, essentially a comedy, expanding on the chronicle initially entered in the Stationers' Register dated 7 February 1603, announced at its first publication, and still suggested in its new title. Nor does his blurb hint of "TRAGEDIE," the folio's label and suggestion in irresolute placement of the play, in the vast majority of copies, right after the last of the histories, *Henry VIII*, and right before the first of the tragedies, *Coriolanus*. There are neither so much as an entry in the table of contents nor page numbers. So the "Never Writer"'s introduction indicates that *Troilus and Cressida* is another problem play betwixt and between—with *All's Well That Ends Well* and *Measure for Measure*—akin to those of the other troubling satiric comedies, atonal what-you-wills notable for their witty, manipulative play with language and logic, plot and situation, economics and politics, society and psyche by Marston, Jonson, Middleton, Chapman, and others, which dominated the London stage during the transition from Elizabeth to James.

Rhetorical display and generic and tonal mixture indicate the same witty purpose. Whatever else the "Never Writer to the Ever Reader" may be doing in his advertisement for *Troilus and Cressida*, there can be no doubt that he promotes the attraction of wit for a purchaser. A further question roused by this letter issues from the very printing of this text and blurb. Since in 1605 Jonson's *Sejanus, his Fall* was elaborately produced to gain revenue specifically as a reading text, since *Troilus and Cressida* is third only to *Hamlet* and *King Lear* in length, since no evidence exists of any contemporary production, and since few productions followed across the next several centuries, scholars have speculated that *Troilus and Cressida*'s publisher might have designed a reading text more than a performance script.[2]

Certainly reading provides a surer way for an audience to catch the conceited wit touted by the blurb. The "Never Writer" leaves little doubt what sorts of rhetorical figures he deems demonstrate such wit. To tote up references to "wit," there are "a birth of your brain that never undertook anything comical vainly," "this author's comedies . . . showing such a dexterity and power of wit" that those "heavy-witted worldlings as were never capable of the wit of a comedy . . . have found that wit there that they never found in themselves, and have parted better witted . . . feeling an edge of wit set upon them," "so much and such savoured salt of wit is in his comedies," "none more witty than this," "And so I leave all such to be prayed for—for the states of their wits' healths—that will not praise it." Even ignoring the many reinforcing references to comedy initiated by "passing full of the palm comical" and disregarding the antithetical pairings that imply "wit" in opposition to "will," "pleasure," and "judgement," the "Ever Reader" can make no mistake of the focus on wit. Wit distinguishes the author, the play's author, the play, and in useful improvement and sheer pleasure, the reader, merely from the polyptotonic morphing of "wit." Moreover, the repetitions and oppositions in inversions of sound in "Never Writer" with "Ever Reader," puns in "palms" with "palm," jingling alliteration of "never staled with the stage, never clapper-clawed," rimes and near rime of "gravities" with "vanities" that follow "vainly" and "in vain," and other instances reverberate throughout the blurb. Classical references and the juxtaposition of theatrical promotions with antitheatrical prejudices continue to heap up. Making appearances, for example, are the honor of a birth on the waves with Aphrodite and of a surpassing of Terence and Plautus. These comedies the reader in a flattering presumption studied and likely performed. The proffer of *Troilus and Cressida* for scrutiny more than spectacle, for reading and analysis rather than performance, is founded in the supposition that "this author's comedies that are so framed to the life that they serve for the most common commentaries of all the actions of our lives." All is premised on the invaluable combination of the wit of observation with the wit of communication.

Such features, along with the prevalent legal jargon, have led to one other hypothesis, that the play was commissioned for an inns of court production.[3] Whether or not that venue seems tenable, the preponderance of evidence in the introduction targets a primary reading audience of trained professionals who know and appreciate the exhibition of rhetorical skills, or a reading audience who would like to be considered members of that select community of wits.

Precisely because *Troilus and Cressida* focuses on the linkage of wit and reflexivity, that is the display and approbation of observations about personal, social, and political issues, the play has offered grist for a plenitude of studies that thematize and allegorize it in relation to Shakespeare's time, and each critic's. Literary studies from Dryden's revision of the play in 1679 have been deeply disturbed by two issues: Into what genre does the play fall? And what is its tone? Dryden excised and elaborated to make Shakespeare's play conform to tragedy that idealizes heroism and love. His version banishes historical, comical, and satirical presentation that comments on and undercuts these themes; he even disallows the customary presentation of inevitable human failings to live up to such ideals. Critics from the eras of Romanticism through modernism tended to lament or examine the play's splits between tragedy and comedy, between flights of exalted philosophy and bursts of degrading ridicule, or more generally to react to the tone they heard oscillating between passages of Romantic idealism and cynical commentary.[4] A turn from finding the play deeply disturbing because it disrupts ideals to highly informative because it presents contraries and inconsistencies came between G. Wilson Knight in 1930 and Jonathan Dollimore in 1984. Knight's essay in *The Wheel of Fire* was produced with the Depression, Dollimore's brief in *Radical Tragedy* with the provocative combination of disillusion and exhilaration over theoretical critiques of received western European and American beliefs and practices. Knight affirms the superior Trojan pole of the "dualism of (i) immediate and personal experience, intuition, the infinite, the timeless [to] (ii) [the Greek] concepts of order and social system, intellect, the finite world, the time-concept," opposed modes of consciousness grappling specifically within Troilus and perpetually among humanity (72). Dollimore exploits the play's ruptures to claim a decentering, demystifying disintegration of providence and universals, then distributes the locus of consciousness Knight placed in Troilus to many, especially to Cressida (44–50).

Since this shift, *Troilus and Cressida* has offered fertile terrain for stimulating growth through a variety of criticisms. Psychoanalytic and gender critics have opened the play to several perspectives.[5] René Gerard's "The Politics of Desire in *Troilus and Cressida*" has generated lots of response by considering Troilus not so true as callous and sexually exploitative, Cressida as at once shrewdly manipulative and foolish in her failure to follow her own advice, and Pandarus as the mediator of desire. Finally Gerard posits that the play examines the powerful motivation of "mimetic or mediated desire" in love and war, that is, the imitation of and competition with others in sex and in politics. Feminist critics have simultaneously clung to the characterization of Troilus as sexually exploitative and sympathized with Cressida as the victim of a misogynistic patriarchy that denies her any appealing options. Others have followed out the trade in women by extending anthropological paradigms of social operations into market economy and commodity fetishism. Gender critics have not only explored the play's presentation of masculine homosocial and homosexual desires and the abusive use of women, they have also extended critiques of men's competitiveness, its magnification by combat, and warfare's destructiveness. Perhaps the most inciting insights into this complex of themes appear in Barbara E. Bowen's *Gender in the Theater of War: Shakespeare's "Troilus and Cressida"* and its furtherance in Laurie E. Maguire's examination of Diomedes' bullying from the perspective of spouse abuse.[6] Bowen founds her critique on Judith Butler's performativity of gender, Bertolt Brecht's correlations between the theaters of gender and war, and Eve Kosofsky Sedgwick's studies of homosociality and homosexuality. The problem expands through Lars Engle's examination of the play's presentation of arguments over values in a precarious market: "the play illustrates the instability of value markets in a world where there is neither private life . . . nor common life" with the specific consequence that "In *Troilus and Cressida* an ancient code of values is radically demystified by being viewed through the lens of a market economy."[7]

Troilus and Cressida is often seen to comment on, and so become an allegory of its own time, and especially of our own, thereby accounting for a surge of interest beginning with the twentieth century. Eric Mallin views the play as a commentary on "emulation" and consequent factionalism that implicate attempts by Robert Devereux, the Earl of Essex, to become the controlling favorite or to supplant the dying Elizabeth through self-contradictory and vestigial ceremonies of chivalry. For even as her court modulated into early modern social patterns, it remained dependent on a medieval system that simultaneously masked and revealed misogynistic homosociality and homosexuality.[8] Linda Charnes has importantly twice allegorized the play in view of our recent preoccupations, initially with fame or notoriety and individuality, subsequently with willful opportunism.[9] As she puts it, having examined the play first as presenting "the tenuous and tortured relationship between public identity, personal subjectivity, and political historiography in a culture that turns people into commodities and fetishizes famous 'names'" (304), she reconstrues it as presenting "cynical essentialism" or "instrumental stupidity," that "wilfully chosen self-mystification" whereby one argues from a position of belief despite awareness that the belief cannot be sustained (306–9). Both of these studies rely specifically on elaborately formal rhetorical displays and on sophisticated, appreciative audience responses. They depend on the reflexivity of wit.

In sum, all such interpretations are enabled, as Elizabeth Freund influentially demonstrated, by the 1980s' and 1990s' hyperawareness both of critical theory, led by deconstruction, and also of the play's "self-reflecting wit, its heightened language consciousness."[10] Not that *Troilus and Cressida* is unique in attending to, making use of, and analyzing self-reflexive wit. But it does focus to an extraordinary degree on a "rhetoric of citation," of suggestive allusiveness within language and social contexts that enables characters to exhibit and exploit opportunistically, variously and inconsistently, their talk and their situations until they themselves become citations of multitudinous, conflicting potentials that have proved psychologically disturbing, and semantically generative. The conditions of a reflexivity that affirms wit in performance and in reception are what I want to reconsider. For these conditions enable the host of potent themes that *Troilus and Cressida* inevitably continues to stimulate.

The formal bases of stylistic rhetoric make it useful for analytic descriptions of how multiple potential meanings can be arrayed to gain audience affirmation. And *Troilus and Cressida* offers an apt test. For it self-consciously presents the reflexivity of wit, that is, various speakers' verbal displays and manipulations, complete with an appreciative audience's corroborations and interactions as both join together in affirming personal, social, and political positions. A brief elaboration of bases set in the play for Ulysses' straightforward manipulation of Achilles suggests why this rhetoric is potentially useful.

It is significant that, while Ulysses has set up the Greek warriors' parade so as to snub Achilles ("pass strangely by him / As if he were forgot. . . . / Lay negligent and loose regard upon him" [3.3.41]), he does not introduce the notion of reflexivity to Achilles. He just manipulates Achilles' contemplation of the reflexivity of the situation: "I have derision medicinable / To use between your strangeness and his pride, / Which his own will shall have desire to drink" (44–46). When Ulysses comes up, Achilles has already been calculating the importance of reflexivity to self-esteem and analyzing its potential lessons for his new situation, perhaps his loss of status. After initial astonishment, he acknowledges the exceeding importance of the general proposition of regarding one's self through one's perception of how others regard one:

> 'Tis certain greatness, once fall'n out with fortune,
> Must fall out with men too. What the declined is,
> He shall as soon read in the eyes of others
> As feel in his own fall. . . .
> . . . .

And not man for being simply man
Hath any honour, but honour for those honours
That are without him, as place, riches, and favour—
Prizes of accident as oft as merit,
Which, when they fall, as being slippery standers,
The love that leaned on them, as slippery too,
Doth one pluck down another and together
Die in the fall. (3.3.75–87)

Fixing his meditations on gifts of fortune rather than nature, Achilles recognizes that honors achieved by fortune rather than *vertù*, to borrow Machiavelli's term, are lost with any loss of fortune. Such honors, to reiterate one of the play's repeated terms, come wholly from others. Thus he allows several potential escapes, for honors not yet lost by fortune, honors granted by nature, or honors merited by achievement, a set common in Shakespeare's canon.

"But 'tis not so with me." Achilles pursues the train of thought by trying to apply a lesson drawn from the principle of reflexivity to his own situation. He puzzles over what he arrogantly perceives to be a discrepancy between the general proposition and his personal standing:

Fortune and I are friends: I do enjoy
At ample point all that I did possess,
Save these men's looks, who do methinks find out
Something not worth in me such rich beholding
As they have often given. (3.3.86–92)

But this sudden lack of due observance, the impoverished "beholding" of "these men's looks" now, so disturbs his complacency that in contrast to his earlier disdain he stops Ulysses. Thus Achilles has already confessed his self-esteem's dependence on "reflexivity" before Ulysses manipulates him into recognizing some failings, though not the arrogance from which they issue: "I see my reputation is at stake, / My fame is shrewdly gored" (3.3.228–29).

The significance of the reflexivity acknowledged by Achilles and manipulated by Ulysses has regained considerable purchase through sociological and rhetorical studies from the mid-twentieth century. The basic principle that one's self-esteem is based on one's perception about how others perceive one provides a corollary to the general theory of "symbolic interactionism" formulated by George Herbert Mead, then extended by famous micro-sociological studies of role-playing by Erving Goffman, scarifying social psychological experiments in role-playing by Philip G. Zimbardo, and sophisticated theorizing from Peter L. Berger and Thomas Luckmann through Pierre Bourdieu to Anthony Giddens.[11] For all of its complex potential consequences and applications, the basic notion seems almost too commonplace. But it does require some surrender of the notion of essential or real selves to selves constructed through social traditions, interactions, adaptations and inventions, whether these be seen as deterministic or open to agency. So, granted the postulate of a reflexivity of self-esteem, a test of its operation in *Troilus and Cressida* rests on the examination of displays of self in speeches wherein speakers seek others' recognition and thus affirmation of self-estimates. This examination depends in turn on stylistic analysis of speeches made to audiences, along with the conditions of their presentations and their consequences. It falls into the domain of formal rhetorical analysis. Specifically it establishes a remarkable concord with the fundamental issue of rhetoric—appeal to an audience, traditionally by rationality, emotion, and identification or ethos.

To return, then, to the 1609 letter and the emphasis on Pandarus, whose name memorializes his deed, is to foreground witty displays of self and calculation that have long adhered to another name, what I call the wit of Ulysses, as well as to interplays of wit among characters, what I call the wit of Pandarus, along with a counter commentary of scurrility, what I call the wit of Thersites. This is not to say that characters other than those for whom the modes are named do not employ these varieties of wit. At various times different characters use each kind. In fact, my argument depends on their general availability. Nor will my division seem strikingly new. For example, Bowen describes stylistic pairings of characters who leap from personal observations to general abstractions, magnify specifics into universals, with their converse who reduce or fragment wholes into parts, contract universals into personal, devaluing specifics (76–77). Her pairing corresponds roughly to the wit displays of Ulysses versus those of Thersites. Likewise, T. McAlindon assesses *Troilus and Cressida* as an exhibit of violations of decorum appropriate for speaker, listeners, subject, and situation that represent disfigurations of souls; he suggests that this same contrast comes between "surplusage," excess gravity in "bomphiologia," bombast, and "diminishing," "tapinosis," Puttenham's "abbaser."[12] Similarly this division between the display wit of Ulysses and the scurrilous wit of Thersites could be considered as the two poles of epideictic, *laus* and *vituperatio*, praise and blame, eulogy and satire. Or it might be expressed by clashes between the idealizations of Ulysses and the demystifications of Thersites, perhaps in the universally attested spectrum of distinctive usages in Bakhtinian descriptions of heteroglossia.[13] In another similar vein, the wit of Pandarus could be epitomized as the self-advertising, slick badinage of the social broker who oils a community's wheels.

Displays of Self and Calculation, or the Wit of Ulysses

The wit of Ulysses appears in two related guises. One shows off to gain credence and identification; the other exploits that credibility and identification through analysis and manipulation to the speaker's advantage. Display has as well been labeled "game," "parody," most aptly "spectacle," at its most obvious "emptied ritual" by Lawrence Danson.[14] Calculation, both in analysis and in proposal, a trait ever associated with Ulysses, might usefully be considered Machiavellism. Display leads to calculation in Ulysses' initial scene with the Greek council. He first delivers the set piece about degree. Then he follows up with a sniping analysis of the disruptive actions of Achilles' entourage and, after Aeneas's interruption bearing Hector's challenge, with a plan of action for Nestor. Both display and calculation focus and depend on recognition and approval by an appreciative, compliant, helping audience.

Significantly overlooked by most commentators is the fact that Ulysses' famous expression of the received exaltation of degree before his Greek comrades in arms, his mode of self-display, opens in homage to and concludes with dependence for success on the applause of those to whom it pays obeisance—the commander in chief, Agamemnon, and the bearer of ancient wisdom, Nestor. Audience recognition is especially important for exhibition speeches, broadly recognized idealizations of a culture's self-estimation, for they depend on the visible, vocal appreciation of a prominent audience. Thus Ulysses begins with a string of epithets characterizing the "great commander, nerve and bone of Greece . . . soul and only spirit" who ought to encompass all the Greeks, along with his senior counselor "most reverend for thy stretched-out life," whose preceding speeches are endowed with the authority of brass and the wisdom of silver (1.3.55–58, 60, 64–65). Though Dawson's note suggests that Ulysses' opening excesses of balanced deference may indicate ironic parody, more likely they serve as the honor of imitation and the guidance of his chief audience's reciprocal response to his forthcoming set piece. For that is what he earns. Nestor pronounces, "Most wisely hath Ulysses here discovered / The fever whereof all our power is sick." Then Agamemnon encourages Ulysses to proceed to specific analysis of the situation he has declared to be in violation of the principles generally honored in word if denied in deed: "The nature of the sickness found, Ulysses, / What is the remedy?" (1.3.139–42).

The degree speech embodies a prominent and broadly received idealization of the hierarchical order of nature as a pattern for social success. Thereby following Aristotle's fundamental proposition about deliberative speech, it emanates from the "contingent" and the "probable" that Dilip Parmeshwar Gaonkar insightfully labels "a generalized social epistemology" of the usual, the normal on which formulation of prudent public decisions relies.[15] Thus Ulysses' principle for success, and through the applause of Agamemnon and Nestor the Greek council's, is to affirm in action as well as precept the presumably hierarchical natural order of the universe so as to gain the social cohesion necessary to defeat the Trojans. The principle's relatively widespread appearance in pronouncements in early modern England—especially in congruent expressions of the often-read Elizabethan homilies "Of Obedience" and "Against Disobedience," Richard Hooker's familiar periods in *Of the Laws of Ecclesiastical Polity*, and elsewhere—is thus exceptionally significant for gauging its immediate effectiveness for the onstage audience.[16]

The rhetorical structure and stylistic devices of the degree speech repetitively embed and multiply reinforce the fundamental principle through amplification. Ulysses' opening sentence states that were it not for Greek failure, Troy would have already fallen. Next he specifies the failing: "The specialty of rule hath been neglected" (1.3.79). The peroration circles back to the exordium in a capping couplet, "To end a tale of length, / Troy in our weakness stands, not in her strength" (1.3.137–38). The remainder of the exordium offers variations on the image and pun that there are as many "hollow" or useless factions among the Greeks as there are tents sheltering the besieging warriors and that various scouting parties are not acting in the venerated concert of a hive of bees. He then elaborates on the primary imagery of cosmic order under the command of the sun, which rightly forms a pattern for social order under a king. "But" he fears how when degree is concealed, natural disasters erupt, and how when hierarchies of age, birthright, abilities and achievements, and so on are disregarded, social disruptions break out. The pattern extolled is one of sustaining harmony versus disturbing discord.

The figures of this speech, from the primary analogical exemplum of cosmos to community, have been reviewed many times over. Its compelling drive derives from a cohesiveness gained by repetitions of an interlocking set of puns and multiplications of near-synonyms, buttressed by parallel phrasing and alliteration. Puns and near-puns echo from the opening "hollow" to the closing, where Troy remains "standing" on "foot" because of all the Greek missteps. "The heavens themselves, [in apposition with the doublet] the planets and this centre / Observe [in a progressive pattern of near-apposition] degree, priority, and place, / Insisture, course, proportion, season, form, / Office, and custom" (1.3.85–88). The sun "corrects" and "posts." The planets, in contrast, wander not through declaration but rather through a sequence of rhetorical questions or "what" exclamations, "What plagues and what portents, what mutiny, / What raging of the sea, [shifting the parallel to the remaining elements] shaking of earth, / commotion in the winds, [and then to nearly synonymous emotional responses] frights, changes, horrors, / [to be succeeded by paired doublets that destroy paired order] divert and crack, rend and deracinate / The unity and married calm of states" (1.3.96–100). Continually the iambic pentameter throb is buttressed by an alliterative "p." All meld to constitute what has often been considered the sonorous rhythms of the passage and I would call its cohesion or integration.

At the climax, as Dawson has emphasized, comes the double *gradatio*, the ladder, series (42–46). Ulysses warns against the strife of supercompetitive ambition where "force" perforce by neglect of degree becomes the sole determinant of a disastrous slippery slope:

> Then everything include itself in power,
> Power into will, will into appetite,
> And appetite, an universal wolf,
> So doubly seconded with will and power
> Must make perforce an universal prey
> And last eat up himself. . . .
> . . . .
> And this neglection of degree it is
> That by a pace goes backward with a purpose
> It hath to climb. The general's disdained
> By him one step below, he by the next,
> That next by him beneath—so every step,

Exampled by the first pace that is sick
Of his superior, grows to an envious fever
Of pale and bloodless emulation. (1.3.119–35)

The horror is doubled by the very ladder of emulation that disregards and disorders the ladder of hierarchical degree that Ulysses had introduced earlier as "the ladder of all high designs" (102).

Diction also contributes to the staid acclaim of the general principle. The degree speech is marked by the extraordinary, innovative diction that is generally considered characteristic of *Troilus and Cressida*, that is a hallmark of problem comedies since Marston, and that particularly marks this style of self-display. It features, for instances, "mastic," "insisture," "deracinate," "fixure," "dividable," "primogenity," "mere oppugnancy." Neologisms and the preponderance of nominalized verbs throughout add to the gravity, the weight of significant support of prudent public decisions.

Consequently the effect on the audience on stage is approval. They seek counsel about the effective application of the principle they have heard extolled. And to this point it seems likely that many of the Jacobeans watching and reading *Troilus and Cressida* were mainly approving. Judging by the elaborate critical attention to the speech over centuries, traditionally Ulysses' degree speech has been considered prudent counsel from Dryden's desire to excavate Shakespeare's "excellent thoughts" from the "heap of Rubbish" through many rhetorical analyses up until the last third of the twentieth century.[17] Perhaps a cynical young inns of court and courtier audience, or aspirants to such status, were more skeptical.

Judged by recent critical attention, the final effect of Ulysses and of *Troilus and Cressida*, following the tendency of problem plays, is modulation into an undercutting, a demystification, a deconstruction of the initial effect. This ironic self-correction has been labeled "retrospective parody" by Yachnin (55). One example cited by Dawson is the oration's use of the same image, the ladder, for the overweening ambition or "emulation" condemned as well as the "degree" praised. An audience seems to be called to reconsider the favorable initial view of hierarchy as the clamber to gain hierarchical status converts to strife. But the primary retrospective reflection that shifts perspective comes with Ulysses' Machiavellian mode that manipulates and strategizes in ways that, to most of us now, seem contrary to the idealizations he has just voiced for display.

Ulysses' mode of calculation, that is, analysis of the situation and strategy for action, is still more dependent on audience approval than is his complementary mode of self-display. For the success of his analysis and manipulation depends on moving his audience beyond applause to adherence to his estimate of the situation and then to execution of his plan. Thus he enlists Nestor's participation when he turns to examine and parody Achilles and Patroclus' ridiculing mimicry of Agamemnon's proclamations as fustian, Nestor's ancient wisdom as palsied incompetence, and the strategies of the Greek council as at best inconsequential and at worst cowardly (1.3.142–214). Nestor obligingly supplies the lesson that others imitate Achilles' insolence: "And in the imitation of these twain, / Who as Ulysses says opinion crowns / With an imperial voice, many are infect" (186–88). His catalog of offenders makes way for Ulysses to claim a consequent Greek failure when they rejected unified strategy in favor of individual brute force: "For the great swing and rudeness of his poise, / They place before his hand that made the engine / Or those that with the fineness of their souls / By reason guide his execution" (208–11). Nestor then recaps the moral, "Let this be granted, and Achilles' horse / Makes many Thetis' sons" (212–13).

After Aeneas's interruption, Ulysses asks Nestor to help work out a plan of action based on his previous analysis: "I have a young conception in my brain: / Be you my time to bring it to some shape" (1.3.313–15). Contrary to Nestor's commonsensical predisposition to ask Greece's greatest hero, Achilles, to bear the Greek standard against Hector, the Machiavellian Ulysses proposes that the Greek council turn to Ajax, the monstrous vanity in physique and psyche. Ulysses aims first, to chasten Achilles' infectious arrogance that tempts others into egoistic competition and away from the concerted action necessary to defeat Troy. He aims second, to avoid risking Greek reputation since even if Hector defeats Ajax, the primary Greek hero and honor would remain unblemished. Nestor, at first unable "with his old eyes" (365) to see Ulysses' shrewd device whereby "Blunt wedges rive hard knots" (317), gradually comes to realize that the Machiavel's eye is fixed on the main objectives. Finally approving, "Now Ulysses, I begin to relish thy advice," he immediately begins to spread the plan: "And I will give a taste thereof forthwith / To Agamemnon—go we to him straight." He concludes the scene with an aphorism vulgar in image, tone, and couplet that adumbrate the rhetoric of Thersites, who seems most often to employ Ulysses' mode of calculation:

"Two curs shall tame each other, pride alone / Must tar the mastiffs on as 'twere a bone."

The imagery and figuration of Ulysses' mode of calculation track those of his mode of display but move more directly and analytically. Again Ulysses maintains attention on what is central to the Greek enterprise, the curbing of Achilles' bad example of egoistic enterprise rather than concerted service. That is, he specifically continues within the premise of the degree speech. But now to accomplish his end he attacks Achilles' factionalism with a factionalism that troubles critics for exigently and hypocritically violating his stated principle:

> The seeded pride
> That hath to this maturity blown up
> In rank Achilles must or now be cropped
> Or, shedding, breed a nursery of like evil
> To overbulk us all. (1.3.317–21)

Achilles becomes a fast-growing weed in need of pruning, shaping, domestication, before he seeds a host of weeds instead of an orderly garden, a typical emblem of community prominent in the second Henriad. Once Ulysses has bluntly acknowledged that Hector's challenge is directed specifically at Achilles, he allows to Nestor the figurative elaboration of this interpretation and of its consequence. "Yet in the trial much opinion dwells" (1.3.338), since the result of the duel of champions will be seen to represent the final outcome of the conflict between Greeks and Trojans. So its effect on morale could amount to a self-fulfilling prophecy. But Ulysses adheres to the central issue by, like many other calculating leaders in Shakespeare and prefiguring the Trojan debate over values, comparing this decision to that of planning a business venture:

> let us like merchants
> First show foul wares and think perchance they'll sell:
> If not,
> The lustre of the better shall exceed
> By showing the worse first. (1.3.357–61)

Then he can calculate the consequences of the duel: If Achilles were to win he would arrogantly refuse to share glory with the Greek forces, yet if he loses all would be besmirched in his defeat. In either case the Greek cause suffers. On the other side, the choice of Ajax will certainly help purge Achilles of egoism. Moreover, if Ajax wins, the medicine will be the stronger, whereas if he loses the Greek army remains untouched. Not only does Ulysses' plan avoid the problems Nestor foresees, his plan attacks the problem that all have agreed blocks Greek success: "hit or miss, / Our project's life this shape of sense assume: / Ajax employed plucks down Achilles' plumes" (1.3.384–85). The plan guarantees success.

The figures of this mode point to as well as support analytic processes: the plan to eliminate weeds and establish an orderly garden, the calculation of projected losses and gains, the prognosis and prescription to purge a surfeit of ego. While the figures, schemes, and diction of Ulysses' mode of calculation are restrained in contrast to those of his mode of display, they function efficiently and effectively at critical moments in the argument. So do these in the initial establishment of the self-characterizing strategy and in the concluding homely figured and aphoristic capping couplet. Moreover, Ulysses' modes often work, as they do here, in concert. He employs them often. And so do others.

Ulysses' style of self-display in winning adherence is prominent on political and social occasions that combine ceremony with deliberation, such as his speeches in the Greek council and his address on reflexivity at the end of the promenade to snub Achilles. This style featuring vivid figuration, striking, innovative diction, and paired near synonyms, however, is introduced by Agamemnon's initial address and Nestor's following application of its thesis. Agamemnon announces the topics to be deliberated by Greek leaders, the reasons underneath frustrations and discouragements across years of failure besieging Troy and the potential responses to the situation:

> checks and disasters
> Grow in the veins of actions highest reared,
> As knots, by the conflux of meeting sap,
> Infects the sound pine and diverts his grain,
> Tortive and errant, from his course of growth. (1.3.5–9)

This style Nestor replicates in his application of the principle introduced by Agamemnon, that "In the reproof of chance / Lies the proof of men" (33–34). His wordplay on "proof" of "valour's show" versus "valour's worth" and his elaborated conceit of "shallow bauble boats" that show off in still waters but flounder in heavy seas modulate through a series of other figures into an exhortation that the Greeks rise to the challenge. These two speeches Dawson's note labels as "full of windy rhetoric and circumlocution, with simple ideas weighed down by abstraction and tortured expression" (95). They signal a slide from *Rhetorica ad Herennium*'s "grave style" into a "bloated" one. This style of display appears as well in Aeneas's courtliness, particularly when he continues the tone but changes the topic of the Greek council by announcing Hector's challenge (1.3.216–310). The same tone, albeit in debate rather than pronouncements and analyses, is again evident in the parallel Trojan council scene (2.2).[18] It forms the dominant discourse of the idealizing and rationalizing that go on when councils deliberate and speakers promulgate political pronouncements epitomized by one facet of Ulysses' wit.

Similarly, Ulysses' style of calculation makes its appearance elsewhere besides his own deployment of it during the Greek council. Observing that Achilles has won Thersites from Ajax, Ulysses opens a series of analytic comments with the aphoristic personifications and image that "The amity that wisdom knits not, folly may easily untie" (2.3.90); then he makes use of these observations to puff up Ajax. Again he uses the style to instruct the Greek leaders to parade by and ignore Achilles so as to set up the colloquy on reflexivity (3.37 ff.). Most notoriously he uses it to evaluate Cressida: "There's language in her eye, her cheek, her lip, / Nay her foot speaks, her wanton spirits look out / At every joint and motive of her body. . . . [setting her down as one of the] sluttish spoils of opportunity / And daughters of the game" (4.5.55–63).

Other characters also employ the calculating style in their estimates of others and of situations. The earliest comes when Troilus sums up the status of the long siege of Troy in lines that forecast the controversy over value:

> Fools on both sides, Helen must needs be fair
> When with your blood you daily paint her thus.
> I cannot fight upon this argument,
> It is too starved a subject for my sword. (1.1.84–87)

Cressida's soliloquy confessing attraction to Troilus after her early banter with Pandarus ends in a set of calculating proverbial couplets that she applies to her own situation:

Women are angels, wooing:
Things won are done, joy's soul lies in the doing;
That she belov'd knows nought that knows not this:
Men prize the thing ungained more than it is;
That she was never yet that ever knew
Love got so sweet as when desire did sue.
Therefore this maxim out of love I teach:
Achievement is command, ungained beseech.
Then though my heart's content firm love doth bear,
Nothing of that shall from mine eyes appear. (1.2.246–55)

Agamemnon employs the calculating style to dress down Patroclus and Achilles when Achilles tries to shun his official call (2.3.100–127). Achilles employs it to evaluate his situation just before and then during Ulysses' reflexivity ruminations (3.3.75–93ff). Diomedes, traditionally Ulysses' double, proves to be another master of the calculating style when he evaluates the situation of the siege and later assesses and bullies Cressida and Troilus in the last scenes. Even Priam employs it during the Trojan council when, complete with couplets, common analogies, and aphoristic point, he accuses Paris of self-service in his vow to defend Helen: "Paris, you speak / Like one besotted on your sweet delights: / You have the honey but these the gall, / So to be valiant is no praise at all" (2.2.142–45).

A distinctive problem for tonal assessments arises from each of Ulysses' two styles of discourse. The first is the retrospective reconsideration that undercuts when Ulysses or his shadows seem in calculation and manipulation to act in ways contrary to ideals they have just expressed, witness the Greek council scene. Thence issues a long heritage of critiques, epitomized when in her introduction to the play Jane Adamson accuses Ulysses of such discrepancies between preachments and practices that he calls into question all propositions he invokes.[19] The other follows from another long critical tradition summed up in Parker's comprehensive indictment of the obverse side of "dilation" or "inflation." The consequences range from "blown up" flatulence to a physical and moral cancer or infected tumor. Moreover, all these she associates with a range of styles that accrue taint in the problem plays of the War of the Theaters (220–27). Ulysses' complementary styles offer the largest potential evaluative scope of the three primary styles in *Troilus and Cressida*.

Interactive Verbal Sparring, or the Wit of Pandarus

The verbal sparring, banter, or wit of Pandarus might be considered brokerage or, somewhat less disparagingly, the wit of social grease or social facilitation. Its reflexivity differs from that of Ulysses' as it is neither primarily display, though the parties must show appreciation of each others' remarks for it to be effective, nor is it calculation, though it makes suggestions and observations and it calculatingly misunderstands so as to play off understandings. Above all, more than Ulysses' style, or Thersites,' it requires reciprocity, back-and-forth talk. It recalls stichomythia between two characters thrusting and parrying with words and phrases, though it seems less schematic and it depends more on puns, language games, and intentional mistakings so as to tease and play. Pandarus's style is the least discussed of the three dominant stylistic modes in *Troilus and Cressida* even though his is the witty comic style that the writer of the 1609 letter commends.

Pandarus's wit predominates in the opening and in love scenes, but it fades as the play concentrates more on war and darker moods until he presents his epilogue of couplets that is different from his earlier prose give-and-take but akin to his song for Paris and Helen. His wit introduces both Troilus and Cressida. In their banter Troilus falls from his customary exalted albeit physical flights of courtly wooing into Pandarus's wit. For the impatient lover needs to respond to his broker's demand for more patience yet ("I'll not meddle nor make no farther: he that will have a cake out of the wheat must tarry the grinding") by countering, "Have I not tarried?" (1.1.13–16). This leads into the sequenced *gradatio* on baking, interrupted by the parallel protests based on "tarry," that Bevington notes sound sexually suggestive:

> PANDARUS Ay, the grinding, but you must tarry the bolting.
>
> TROILUS Have I not tarried?
>
> PANDARUS Ay, the bolting, but you must tarry the leavening.
>
> TROILUS Still have I tarried.
>
> PANDARUS Ay, to the leavening; but here's yet in the word hereafter the kneading, the making of the cake, the heating of the oven, and the baking; nay, you must stay the cooling too or you may chance to burn your lips. (1.1.17–24)

Characteristic is the building of a *gradatio* that develops a homely conceit in a sexually suggestive way, based on parallels in phrasing and repetitions of words or word roots that shift quickly so as to convey a memorable, easy transit rather than an inflexible scheme. All contribute to the effect of constant interchange (even in Pandarus's longer statement Troilus is permitted visual though no verbal protest). Pandarus goes on to typically suggest Cressida's sexual attraction by refusing as her uncle to mention it. This mode of *occupatio* emphasized by contradictives elicits Troilus's extended praise. Then he pretends teasingly that Troilus is not enamored, worse that Troilus remains unappreciative of his efforts as go-between, taking now as his catch words, "between," "kin," "fair." He thereby continues to inflame Troilus's anticipation.

Cressida's first appearance, asking her servant Alexander about the progress of the war, provides him opportunity to display a satiric, stylized wit about Ajax's clumsiness, bestiality, and ill-composition ("he hath the joints of everything, but everything so out of joint" [1.2.23–24]). This scoffing prepares for Pandarus arriving and engaging his niece in an extended interactive display of social wit marked by courtly *sprezzatura*. As he whetted Troilus's appetite for Cressida by the pretense that it was insufficiently hearty, so he tries to augment Cressida's interest in Troilus by making comparisons to other heroes and noting Troilus's attractiveness to other women. In response she pretends that Troilus is deficient and draws ridiculous conclusions that contradict her uncle's obvious intentions. The game begins over the anger in Hector's challenge to the Greeks and Pandarus's comparison of Troilus's prowess to Hector's. "Troilus will not come far behind him, let them take heed of Troilus" calls forth Cressida's query "What, is he angry too?" (1.2.51, 53). It continues to a stalemate over the intended comparison that denies the possibility of such between the two brothers. It proceeds to Troilus's qualities (indescribable because excessive in Pandarus's speech that is "true and not true"), Helen's love for Troilus ("Then she's a merry Greek indeed"), and Troilus proving to be an "old lifter" (thief and fornicator rather than muscle man [1.2.85, 95, 103]). This series of hyperbolic spins, wordplay, and mistakings of intent conclude in Pandarus's example of Troilus's display of wit and Cressida's response that he should let the tale "pass" "for it has been a great while going by" (1.2.144, 145).

As they watch the heroes return to the city walls, Pandarus offers praise and tries to return to the topic of Troilus until Cressida asks, "What sneaking fellow comes yonder?" (1.3.192). Pandarus's praise of Troilus by eulogistic commonplaces that "season a man" Cressida translates into "a minced man, and then to be baked with no date in the pie, for then the man's date is out" (1.3.217–19). Less submerged come the concluding bawdry, catching wordplay on watch and ward, applications of domains of defense in fencing and fortification, and balanced parallel phrases based on parison and its modifications:

> PANDARUS You are such a woman—a man knows not at what ward you lie.
>
> CRESSIDA Upon my back to defend my belly, upon my wit to defend my wile, upon my secrecy to defend mine honesty, my mask to defend my beauty, and you to defend all these; and at all these wards I lie, at a thousand watches.
>
> PANDARUS Say one of your watches.
>
> CRESSIDA Nay, I'll watch you for that, and that's one of the chiefest of them too. If I cannot ward what I would not have hit, I can watch you for telling how I took the blow, unless it swell past hiding and then it's past watching. (1.3.220–30)

Pandarus's scene with Paris and Helen, aimed at concealing Troilus and Cressida's well-known affair, completes his final task in the role of sexual broker and constitutes his other extended display of the wit characterized in the 1609 blurb. It too opens with an overture, of another clever servant's domain switching puns, until Pandarus concludes that "we understand not one another. I am too courtly and thou too cunning" (3.1.26–27). This witplay introduces the musical refrain—with "parts," "good broken music," "harmony," "performance," "melody," and so on—that echoes all along and crescendos in Pandarus's impromptu bawdy song. Music suggests an atmosphere of love play as the trio of Pandarus, Paris, and Helen continue to improvise clever variations on catch words that flow back and forth. "Fair" with "rude," "sweet," and "love" culminate in the same ostensibly extempore lyric, "Love, love, nothing but love, still love, still more!" (1.3.99). In turn this stimulates Paris's generatively patterned love patter: "He eats nothing but doves, love, and that breeds hot blood, and hot blood begets hot thoughts, and hot thoughts beget hot deeds, and hot deeds is love" (3.1.112–14). Subsequently Pandarus greases wittily to tease Cressida the morning after the lovers' only tryst (4.2) before the Greeks arrive to fetch her to her father. Then his stylistic mode modulates into testiness over Troilus's insistence that Cressida "be true" as she is being escorted away (4.2).

As obvious from the witty overtures in the duet with Cressida and the trio with Helen and Paris, Pandarus's wit is necessarily employed by others as well as the broker for whom it is named. Cressida and the Greeks use the mode when she arrives at the Greek camp (4.5.15ff). The heroes often employ it during periods of truce to engage in homosocial bonding through competition. Just so Aeneas meets Diomedes on the arrival of Cressida's Greek escorts:

> AENEAS Health to you, valiant sir,
> During all question of the gentle truce;
> But when I meet you armed, as black defiance
> As heart can think or courage execute.
>
> DIOMEDES The one and other Diomed embraces.
> Our bloods are now in calm and, so long, health!
> But when contention and occasion meet,
> By Jove I'll play the hunter for thy life
> With all my force, pursuit, and policy.
>
> AENEAS And thou shalt hunt a lion that will fly
> With his face backward.... (4.1.11–21)

Achilles and Hector employ a harsher version in the Greek camp after the duel (4.5.230ff). And Agamemnon, Nestor, and Ulysses parody the mode in order to simultaneously flatter, manipulate, and ridicule Ajax, at least insofar as Ajax can keep up his part (2.3.130ff). The socially lubricating wit of Pandarus, understandably, offers the widest-ranging set of ends and timbres of these three sorts.

Scurrilous EnCounters, or the Wit of Thersites

As verbal skirmish, the wit of Thersites is similar to Pandarus's reciprocal and reflexive wit of social grease. As evaluation, it is similar to Ulysses' wit of calculation. But it is starkly different from the others in its distinctively narrow timbre of vituperative scurrility. Critics have long described this style as the foremost contributor to *Troilus and Cressida*'s tone of disillusionment. Thersites' talk has been labeled "railery," "cynicism," "envy" with "prurience" and "coarseness" or "grossness," "degradation," "debunking," "demystification."[20] Particularly interesting is a line that follows Rosalie Colie who, working from traditions of mock encomium to characterize *Troilus and Cressida* through Thersites, focuses on two of his rhetorical techniques.[21] The first is the reduction of characters to self-referential names. This appears not only in the marquee acts of Troilus, Cressida, and Pandarus but also in the popular Ajax pun, in Patroclus as masculine whore, and in Thersites himself as bastard (333–38). The second mark of Thersites' railing is fragmentation and atomization (341–45). This observation links many who have called to attention the imagery of disease that dominates Thersites' speech and becomes the pervasive "dilation" of bloated, diseased bodies examined by Parker (220–28). This "matter" of Thersites and *Troilus and Cressida* has been associated with images of waste through Thersites' attack on Ajax as privy and then more generally with Bakhtinian carnivalesque laughter at fundament by Bruce Boehrer.[22] In brief, the wit of Thersites indicates an array of means for abusively debunking idealization.

From opening to closing Thersites rails on—initially in scurrilous enCounters or flytings of Ajax rather like Hal's contests with Falstaff, except these rend. Partly this results from the contest between wit and half-wit. Mainly, however, it derives from Thersites' tone, as he sustains it against Achilles and Patroclus as well. In his first appearance, suffering a beating by Ajax for refusing to pay attention, Thersites alternately compares the stupidity of his master to irrational animals and curses Ajax's physical superiority. He counters Ajax's declaration that he "will beat thee into handsomeness" with, "I shall sooner rail thee into wit and holiness," then adds, "but I think thy horse will sooner con an oration than thou learn a prayer without a book," and finally offers an imprecation to demonstrate the gap between humanity and the equine Ajax, "A red murrain o'thy jade's tricks" (2.1.11–16). He counters Ajax's command to recount the proclamation of Hector's challenge, "Thou art proclaimed a fool I think," then fantasizes retaliation to threats of more beatings, "I would thou didst itch from head to foot and I had the scratching of thee: I would make thee the loathsomest scab in Greece" (20–23). When Ajax calls him names, Thersites declares Ajax a domestic animal, "thou sodden-witted lord, thou hast no more brain than I have in mine elbows: an asinico may tutor thee. Thou scurvy valiant ass, thou art here but to thrash Trojans, and thou art bought and sold among those of any wit like a barbarian slave" (38–41). Ajax is an outhouse; a fool would shame his wit; "There's

Ulysses and old Nestor, whose wit was mouldy ere your grandsires had nails on their shoes, yoke you like draught oxen and make you plough up the wars" (95–97). Later he shifts his attack to Patroclus and Achilles for trying to muzzle him. Achilles holds his own far better, and Patroclus somewhat better, than Ajax in their scurrilous enCounters with Thersites. Achilles initially attacks his newly acquired fool as a "cur of envy," a "crusty botch of nature," and a "fragment," but Thersites counters "thou picture of what thou seem'st, and idol of idiot worshippers," and "full dish of fool" (5.1.5–10). Patroclus gains a curse as Achilles' "masculine whore" for appreciating Thersites' wit: "Now the rotten diseases of the south, the guts-griping, ruptures, catarrhs, loads o'gravel in the back, lethargies, cold palsies . . . take and take again such preposterous discoveries" (5.1.17–22).

More memorable than Thersites' flytings of wit are his imaginative assessments. He is as masterful as Ulysses in calculation, just as he is as adept as Pandarus in encounter. He contrasts to both in scurrility. His most frequent targets are the stupidity of the master he deserts, Ajax (2.3.1ff.; 3.3.250ff.), and the one he joins, Achilles with his appendage Patroclus. One of his catechisms reaches a preliminary climax in a declension of the Greeks' martial hierarchy, "Agamemnon commands Achilles, Achilles is my lord, I am Patroclus' knower, and Patroclus is a fool" to reach a greater climax in a progressive parison and *gradatio*: "Agamemnon is a fool to offer to command Achilles, Achilles is a fool to be commanded of Agamemnon, Thersites is a fool to serve such a fool, and Patroclus is a fool positive" (2.3.46–48, 55–57). Another of Thersites' frequent targets is the war. For example, he calls down venereal disease on the combatants, the "Neapolitan bone-ache, for that methinks is the curse depending on those that war for a placket" (2.3.15–16). And, in frequently quoted lines, he debunks heroism: "Here is such patchery, such juggling, and such knavery: all the argument is a whore and a cuckold—a good quarrel to draw emulous factions and bleed to death upon. Now the dry serpigo on the subject, and war and lechery confound all!" (2.3.63–66). Thus he degrades or at least he proclaims the degradation of both great traditional literary themes, heroism and love, that Dryden sought to elevate again in his reformation of *Troilus and Cressida*.

Thersites makes devastating summations of the failings of Greek heroes and he assesses at once the consequences of the love triangle. His opening offers a tantalizing preview and epitome of this mode. Punctuated by Ajax's calls, he is considering the failures of the Greek commander analogized as a repellant infection, decked in multilayered puns on command and widespread application, on oozing and fleeing, on center and heart, corpus, and corpse, and on substantial action or reason and pus: "Agamemnon, how if he had boils—full, all over, generally . . . And those boils did run—say so—did not the general run then, were not that a botchy core. . . . Then would come some matter from him, I see none now" (2.1.2–8). Later, evaluating all the leaders, he becomes somewhat more expansive, remains every bit as reductive. After recalling Achilles's and Patroclus's excessive passion and defective reason, he turns punningly to the overeating and whoring of the commander Agamemnon, the cuckolding of his brother and deputy Menelaus, and the stupidity of both: "Here's Agamemnon, an honest fellow enough and one that loves quails, but he has not so much brain as earwax, and the goodly transformation of Jupiter there, his brother, the bull, the primitive statue and oblique memorial of cuckolds" (5.1.48–50). Viewing the Greek gathering later, Thersites heaps disdain on Nestor and Ulysses, the wise old and the shrewd young heads of the Greek council, because the political scheme they devised and carried out so as to gain martial order and victory has resulted in greater disorder than before. Prudent strategy is fallen into as ill repute as stupidity in a dog-eat-dog world:

> Now they are clapper-clawing one another, I'll go look on. . . . the policy of those crafty swearing rascals—that stale old mouse-eaten dry cheese, Nestor, and that same dog-fox, Ulysses—is proved not worth a blackberry: they set me up in policy that mongrel cur, Ajax, against that dog of as bad a kind, Achilles, and now is the cur Ajax prouder than the cur Achilles and will not arm today; whereupon the Grecians begin to proclaim barbarism and policy grows into an ill opinion. (5.4.1–13)

Thersites' dissection of the love triangle appropriately comes in snippets as, observing Ulysses and Troilus spying on Diomedes and Cressida in the Greek camp, he comments on their reactions. In a favorite Shakespeare scenario of ironically encompassing overwatchings, when Ulysses suggests that Cressida "will sing any man at first sight," Thersites bawdily chimes in puns unheard by the pair: "And any man may sing her, if he can take her clef: she's noted" (5.2.9–11). He contributes such memorably vicious comic sneers over love pathos as the darkly figurative "How the devil Luxury with his fat rump and potato finger tickles these together. Fry, lechery, fry!" and the couplet "A proof of strength she could not publish more, / Unless she said 'My mind is now turned whore'" before he sums up the scene, "Lechery, lechery, still wars and lechery, nothing else holds fashion—a burning devil take them" (5.2.55–56, 112–13, 191–93).

Thersites is expert in providing scurrilous analytic choral digests, even in assaying himself. Surprised by Hector's challenging question, "art thou for Hector's match? / Art thou of blood and honour?" he proves as self-knowing as self-loathing in his self-protection: "No! No, I am a rascal, a scurvy railing knave, a very filthy rogue" (5.4.22–25). He similarly anatomizes his status with the multiple play on "bastard" when challenged by Margarelon:

> I am a bastard too, I love bastards! I am bastard begot, bastard instructed, bastard in mind, bastard in valour, in everything illegitimate. One bear will not bite another, and wherefore should one bastard? Take heed, the quarrel's most ominous to us: if the son of a whore fight for a whore, he tempts judgement. (5.8.7–11)

Though the master of the scurrilous wit of enCounter and the demeaning commentator on *Troilus and Cressida*, Thersites is not inimitable either in insulting and cursing skirmishes or in degrading analyses of love and war. Troilus's early love-smitten cry for peace and analysis of the war over little more than pride partakes almost as much of Thersites as of Ulysses (1.1.84–88). Diomedes' bitter response to Paris's question, "Who in your thoughts deserves fair Helen best, / Myself or Menelaus?" partakes more of Thersites than of Ulysses:

> He like a puling cuckold would drink up
> The lees and dregs of a flat tamed piece;
> You like a lecher out of whorish loins
> Are pleased to breed out your inheritors.
> Both merits poised, each weighs nor less nor more,
> But he as he, the heavier for a whore. (4.1.62–67)

Formal Reflections

One critical employment of the Trojan council on value is it sets up an epitome of uses for formal rhetorical, here mainly stylistic, analysis. Kenneth Palmer has described how the Trojan council follows a pattern similar to that of the earlier Greek council and how juxtaposition of the pair sets the ideological context of *Troilus and Cressida* (41). In the Greek council, under Ulysses' guidance, the affirmation of faith and "serious diagnosis of ills and their cure has declined by the end into mere chicanery" (45). At base, like the Greek council, the Trojan council also exemplifies the wit of Ulysses: the displays of self in speeches aimed at professions of sociopolitical principles lead to analyses of the current situation, calculations for plans, and applications to gain professed objectives. Beyond the Greek, since the Trojan council constitutes "a true debate, not too far in form from a disputation, with Priam as moderator" (46), it illustrates in addition the interactive and mutually appreciative verbal sparring that marks the wit of Pandarus. Furthermore, at times the Trojan council shifts into the scurrilous evaluations and encounters informed by the wit of Thersites. In whichever of the three modes of witty style, it demonstrates the central focus of self-reflexive and mutually appreciative performance for others. In fact, the outcome of the Trojan council's debate over "value" that has constituted critical tradition's preoccupation in *Troilus and Cressida* is determined by the Trojan desire for "honor," that is evaluating and appreciating themselves as they see themselves being evaluated and appreciated by others. So, in the final analysis, the Trojan council chiasmically crosses the Greek, beginning in calculation and concluding in the affirmation of the chief value of both—not "degree" but "honor."

The council of Troy is convened to respond to the Greek offer of withdrawal if the Trojans return Helen. The question posed is the appropriate evaluation of Helen and thus, presumably, of the motivation for the war between the Greeks and Trojans that has dragged on and drained the blood of martial heroes on both sides. Bevington notes that this question proved a popular one posed for Renaissance rhetorical exhibitions of declamation and debate (361). So Priam's formal opening with its embedded quotation of Nestor's proposal follows the mode of decorous self-exhibition that proposes a mutually agreeable question for deliberation, or calculation, and determination, just as does Agamemnon's proposal that leads to Ulysses' speech on degree. Priam's opening statement is thus filled with the language of rational calculation, analysis, and comparison/contrast for judging the value of Helen with her return against the value of all that has been "consumed / In hot digestion of this cormorant war" (2.2.5–6), a personification of war's ceaseless depletion of resources. Exhausted have been "hours" or "time," "lives" or "friends" along with "wounds," "travail" including "speeches," "expense," plus other factors that go unmentioned but that are "dear," that is, expensive. Hector's response of "Let Helen go" (2.2.17) offers a self-evident response premised on the inherent value of one foreigner versus that of many natives. So begins the calculation, the ledger, the appeal to logos, reason, that ultimately loses during the debate in the Trojan council to the much-discussed appeal to pathos and the less frequently mentioned appeal to ethos. In fact, the trump term for motivation and deliberation based on ethos, "honour," is the first of the "damages" in Nestor's list to be "struck off" if the Trojans return Helen to the Greeks. This observation circles back of course to another of the critical advantages of the Trojan council on value: it offers a gauge of the three traditional appeals of logos, pathos, and ethos on an audience.

Ostensibly there follows a series of appeals to logos that has won extensive critical acclaim (witness the heritage of the Variorum edition) coupled with critical despair over Hector's "victory" in rational terms but his "surrender" for no reason. But for potent motivation. Just so, Helenus makes an appeal to reason. And Hector keeps invoking its self-evidence in terms of calculation. "Brother, she is not worth what she doth cost / The keeping," "But value dwells not in particular will," "'Tis mad idolatry / To make the service greater than the god" (50–51, 53, 56–57) offer parries that lead to his ultimate rational appeal against the pathos of Troilus and Paris:

The reasons you allege do more conduce
To the hot passion of distempered blood
Than to make up a free determination
'Twixt right and wrong. (2.2.168–71)

Hector proceeds (as Palmer describes, 47–48) to make an argument based on the laws of nature and of nations, *ius naturale* and *ius gentium*, that is irrefutable unless the respondent wants to challenge order on behalf of chaos. Thus it is phrased as a rhetorical question and a pair of conclusives that carry the imperative moral force predicated on reason's superiority to passion:

Nature craves
All dues be rendered to their owners: now,
What nearer debt in all humanity
Than wife is to the husband?
. . . .
There is a law in each well-ordered nation

To curb those raging appetites that are
Most disobedient and refractory.
. . . .
Thus to persist
In doing wrong extenuates not wrong,
But makes it much more heavy. (2.2.173–88)

Therefore, "Hector's opinion / Is this in way of truth." Pause.

yet ne'ertheless,
My sprightly brethren, I propend to you
In resolution to keep Helen still,
For 'tis a cause that hath no mean dependence
Upon our joint and several dignities. (2.2.188–93)

Besides its doubled contradictives, Hector's address to "my . . . brethren" signals his allegiance with Troilus and Paris; and his attribution to them of "sprightly" signals his allegiance with pathos and ethos rather than reason and calculation, the logos whereby he has forged his argument. Throughout the debate these contrary bases for debate, pathos and ethos have gathered superior force. That pathos should prove potent can come as little surprise to anyone attending Rebhorn's account of Renaissance rhetoric's valuation of emotional appeals (80–98, 147–61). That ethos is ultimately dominant may seem somewhat surprising initially. But reflection confirms the likelihood. Most Renaissance rhetoricians discussed ethos, often in terms of getting the goodwill of hearers by talking of ourselves versus our enemies during discussions of the exordium under the disposition of parts of an oration. Moreover, Kenneth Burke revitalized the notion of the potency of the ethical appeal, popularizing it under the rubric "identification" in his review and reaffirmation of Aristotelian principles.[23]

Even before Hector presents his appeal to logos in response to Priam's question and Nestor's proposal, he invokes his honor, his reputation in a self-evaluating ethical appeal in response to the opening item in Nestor's calculated listing. "Though no man lesser fears the Greeks than I / As far as toucheth my particular" (2.2.8–9), "yet" because of his care of others he will prudently avoid risking his community's security. Hector's self-evocation based on repute, along with his semi-rhetorical question, "What merit's in that reason which denies / The yielding of [Helen] up?" (2.2.23–24) hands

Troilus opportunity to shift the grounds of the debate. No longer is Helen esteemed for her value in her person, but rather she is to be esteemed for her symbolic value, based ultimately on the estimation of those actions necessary to acquire and defend, essentially to possess her. This shift allows Troilus, seconded by Paris, to devalue reason in many ways and to bring into favor appeals to pathos that ultimately recircle back to appeals to ethos that reaffirm the value of "honor" for all warriors, Greek as well as Trojan. There is in their presentation an underlying logical rebuttal in the argument of waste: they cannot give Helen up without the loss of all their efforts—and consequently the loss of "honor" thereby accruing. This last addition signals that the ultimate appeal that wins the debate is not even pathos but the self-reflexive ethos of reputation.

Throughout the Trojan council victory is prepared for by a continuous devaluation of logos as the instrument for consideration of Helen's value, along with Hector's and Helenus's and Priam's rationales. That devaluation appears by way of a multitude of means in three major movements. First comes Troilus's forthright denigration of reason, his assault on reason as cowardice. Next comes his attempt to appropriate reason to the service and promotion of passion and ethos in a three-part argument dealing with the reason of honor in loyalty to a willed choice, the reason of honor in retribution with enhancing advantage, and the reason of conversion of what might be deemed theft or disgrace into acknowledgment of honorable defense. After Cassandra's interruption and transition, Paris repeats and embellishes these arguments. Finally, all along comes a denigration of reason by means critics have considered characteristic of the style of *Troilus and Cressida*. Such include the reduction of logos to accounting (with values falling to bargains), the reduction of values to easy puns (slides in terminology from rational to sensory suasion) reductions of abstractions to concretions (sometimes physical disorders), and, as a by-product that has come to raise righteous wrath, the reduction of women to possessions, specifically trophies.

Troilus assaults reason as the means of deliberation as soon as Hector's semi-rhetorical question allows others into the debate. Troilus begins with the direct self-contradiction and self-reduction embedded in reason's mere calculations of debits and credits. These represent mean attempts to utilize (in sets of triplets) a "scale" to "weigh" or "counters" to "sum" or "spans" to "buckle in a waist" in terms of "common ounces" or "inches" the invaluable "worth" of regality and "honor" that are "past-proportion," "infinite," "fathomless." Thus in the same terms that characterize Roman versus Egyptian as in *Antony and Cleopatra*, for example, he begins to devalue logos's measurements and suggests the contrasting exaltation of honor that can be evoked only by pathos and ethos. Still more degrading is Troilus's identification of reason with a lack of self-esteem and ambition, resuming the familiar charge Hector had attempted by his ethical appeal to forestall. "Reason flies the object of all harm," swords, and enemies, and the imitation of the father of the gods or a star. Reason serves merely as a euphemism for the evasion of action or cowardice rejected by courage, "manhood and honour."

Then Troilus appropriates reason to buttress a three-part argument based more on passion and ethos when he (in)famously, and successfully, argues the rhetorical question, "What's aught but as 'tis valued?" (2.2.52). He does not suggest, as Hector does, that there may exist a dichotomy between the valuation of something, such as Helen, and some inherent preciousness, or a negotiation between these two poles. Rather, he suggests all along that Helen's value derives from the community's estimate of her, that is, from how much they are willing to sacrifice for her. Essentially her value is determined by reflexiveness, by how each one considers how much others value her. Her value is ascertained by communal valuation, like but beyond the market of calculation he has devalued as a measure since communal valuation depends on emotional involvement, pathos, and self-esteem, ethos.

Troilus takes up Hector's appeal to reason by arguing that reason is servant to constancy of will. Essentially he employs reason to buttress an argument based on an emotional appeal to the value of ethos. His will chooses a wife; then he needs must maintain that will by adhering to this willed choice. To do otherwise would mean to forfeit integrity, to fail "to stand firm by honour" (2.2.68). In logical or accounting terms, this would be the same as purchasing clothing or food and then reneging by asking for an exchange after we have used them. Troilus next employs an analogous historical condition for the rape of Helen by arguing that the Trojans had in advance deliberated rationally and chosen to gain revenge, and then some, for the Greeks keeping in captivity "an old aunt"; in that decision they committed themselves to support Paris's seizure of the beautiful young Helen. This "inestimable" advantage, one beyond calculation, also depends on the premise of an emotional appeal to ethos, especially in its climactic rhetorical question:

Why do you now
The issue of your proper wisdoms rate,
And do a deed that never Fortune did:
Beggar the estimation which you prized
Richer than sea and land? (2.2.88–92)

Troilus's final emotional appeal to ethos that employs reason argues that to return Helen is tantamount to confessing to being thieves, whereas to keep her is essentially to deny the theft and thereby to promote Trojan honor and Greek disgrace. As Palmer points out (46–47), this shifts the grounds on which "honor" is founded. This enthymemic implicature is aggravated by highlighting that the daring rape occurred abroad on Greek soil but that the cowardly surrender would take place in Troy, on home turf. And its impact is emphasized by rhyme:

O theft most base,
That we have stol'n what we do fear to keep;
But thieves unworthy of a thing so stol'n,
That in their country did them that disgrace
We fear to warrant in our native place. (2.2.92–96)

Cassandra's interrupting prophecy that Paris's rape of Helen dooms Troy Troilus disparages. It is an argument from consequences rather than a deliberation on principles. And it represents "brain-sick raptures" rather than "high strains / Of divination" (122, 113–14). He interjects more forcefully still the ethical appeal of "the goodness of a quarrel, / Which hath our several honours all engaged / To make it gracious" and the impassioned appeal that even the "weakest spleen" would stand and fight for such honor (2.2.123–25, 128). Then Paris elaborates the same threefold argument, balked by a momentary interruption and Thersitean chastisement by Priam. He baldly makes an ethical appeal he afterwards reinforces with an emotional call to extend Trojan "generosity" rather than lapse into "degeneracy":

I would have the soil of her fair rape
Wiped off in honourable keeping her.
What treason were it to the ransacked queen,
Disgrace to your great worths and shame to me,
Now to deliver her possession up
On terms of base compulsion? (2.2.148–53)

These arguments based on appropriating logos for pathos and ethos are easily dismissible as the appeals of "hot passion" and "distempered blood" on behalf of "pleasure and revenge" (2.2.169, 171). So Hector dismisses, "Paris and Troilus, you have both said well, / And on the cause and question now in hand / Have glossed, but superficially" (2.2.163–65). Commentators have long belabored the pun obvious from the quarto and folio reading "gloz'd," which acknowledges the commentary but undercuts it with the suggestion of specious rationalization. In this punning dismissal Hector falls in with a set of techniques for reduction employed not on behalf of but instead against rational appeals. Early on in the Trojan council Troilus, when reducing reasoning in the form of calculation, questions encompassing Priam's inestimable honor "With spans and inches so diminutive / As fears and reasons" (2.2.31–32). Helenus counters with a pun annotators have long enjoyed here as with Falstaff in *1 Henry IV*; he makes "reasons" "raisins" through his comment that Troilus will "bite so sharp at reasons" because Troilus has none (33, 35). Troilus then rebuts that Helenus would "fur your gloves with reason. Here are your reasons" (38), which doubles the potential pair of puns he introduced in "fears and reasons," the first of which annotators have failed to appreciate.

A more telling device is the slippage of "will" in Troilus's argument about choosing a wife. "My will" (as Dawson annotates of Aristotelian psychology) should govern passion but is instead "enkindled by mine eyes and ears" (63), which might appear metaphorically to be rational understanding. This reduction is close kin to that of shifting abstractions to concretions. Thereby reason would devalue honor out of fear that makes "livers pale"; ethos and passion rouse courage in the "weakest spleen"; and will becomes stomach for food, passion "distempered blood," and "high strains / Of divination" "brain-sick raptures."

Finally, however deaf earlier critical ears proved to be, more recently outrage has burst out over the offensive reduction of women to possessions. For Hector argues that since the husband is the owner of the wife, the Trojans should return Helen to Menelaus. This increases the volume of criticism of Troilus, which deduces that during his victorious impassioned ethical appeal to masculine honor, Helen's value derives from her serving as a trophy:

She is a theme of honour and renown,
A spur to valiant and magnanimous deeds,

> Whose present courage may beat down our foes
> And fame in time to come canonise us. (2.2.199–202)

All of these techniques that reduce appeals to logos and exalt appeals to pathos, and most of all to ethos, are dedicated to acclaiming "honor" above all other values. Consequently, the Trojan council exalts its own adherence, and implicitly that of Greeks as well, to a sense of masculine self-display and reflexivity based on the opinion of others who count, or on their perceived opinion of others' opinions about themselves. Thus the centrality in *Troilus and Cressida* of Ulysses and Achilles' deliberation about reflexivity, which in turn reaffirms the centrality of the introductory letter from "A Never Writer to an Ever Reader."

Troilus and Cressida makes a contribution to the cluster of problem plays that dominated the era when Elizabeth's England waned and James's waxed, an era of anxiety and hope over difficult, sometimes intransigent oppositions requiring resolution. The linguistic and rhetorical training and the capabilities of the era's elite made witty rhetorical display, admiration, manipulation, interactive communication, exaltation, and vilification at least attractive, perhaps inevitable. And the nature of dramatic presentation with its constraints on authorial intervention and guidance of an audience along with rhetoric's foundation in arguing for all sides of a question, the (in)famous facility to argue *in utramque partem*, made for an extraordinarily propitious presentation of troubled issues in times simultaneously troubled and opportune. Moreover, it opened up problematic plays to conflicting, multiple thematic and allegorical interpretations in later times, especially times that felt likewise compelled to face issues that combine extraordinary potential for both achievement and failure. Rhetorical criticism helps explain how such presentation works.

6

The Rhetorical Advantage

A Retrospective Brief

Anyone who has managed to read this far more or less seriatim apparently considers a formal rhetorical approach useful. Still it might prove helpful to summarize a brief for the position.

The *Measure for Measure* essay depends on a scheme Renaissance rhetoricians were increasingly interpreting as useful for logical argument as well as for entertainment and suasion. Shakespeare employed chiasmus through his plays for all three traditional rhetorical purposes of *delectare et docere et permovere*, offering copious clever self-display and clowning but also effective emphasis on the comparison and contrast of alternative choices. The brief example of chiasmus's use in *2 Henry IV* demonstrates a straightforward reinforcement of the dominant political criterion of royal justice when, in contrast to Falstaff's earlier misuse of the scheme, the newly crowned Henry V declares his choice of the Lord Chief Justice over Falstaff as his adoptive political father. *Measure for Measure* offers a much more complex example of focusing choices based not only on relationships between justice and mercy but also on preferences, equivalences, and values. Here chiasmus is pervasively employed so that it lays out for analysis an array of vexing and perplexing moral and theological, social and political issues. So here, rather than simplifying and rendering perspicuous, the figure increases both the necessity of consideration and the difficulties of resolution by its stark presentation of a set of contentious and intractable issues that seem irresolvable. Thus as history the outcome of the dominant use of chiasmus in *Measure for Measure* would seem to demonstrate the play's prominent membership among Elizabethan-Jacobean problem plays in two ways. First, the play features an ostentatious rhetorical figure. And second, it employs that figure to focus attention on major difficult issues that deeply concerned the era or at least that deeply concern us now in our historical and critical appraisals of that period. As a mode of analysis this formal rhetorical approach reemphasizes the obvious lesson that the employment of a particular rhetorical figure never determines the interpretation of a text since employment of any figure promises a multitude of different potential effects and its analysis offers a multitude of interpretations, dependent on context. Yet I would claim the importance of formal rhetorical criticism as an invaluable point of view both for testing and integrating old interpretations, allegorizations, and also for generating new ones, because the forms determine those contours available for interpretations.

The *All's Well That Ends Well* essay expands consideration to a unit larger than most schemes or tropes, more expansive and more difficult to characterize. Aphorisms provide a crucial form of communication that oral cultures and cultures in transition like the Renaissance depend on to carry a heavy multiple burden. That burden includes communicating the wisdom and prudence of the past, challenging the understanding of the present, interrogating the promise of the future, and proffering a host of potential purposes based in the immediate context of folks employing them. Aphorisms provide means for interaction, entertainment, counsel, and contest. *All's Well That Ends Well* particularly exhibits the dominant use of aphorisms in social contact along with a playful display of enhancing rhetorical trappings of figure and image that together evolve into challenges and counter-challenges, entrapments and counter-entrapments. In doing so the play takes its plotting characteristics from Elizabethan-Jacobean problem comedies, varying that pattern by having for its protagonist not a witty gallant who wins the contest for sexual, social, economic, and political gains, but instead a witty, victorious heroine. Shakespeare exploits the problem comedies' predominant plotting trait of series of surprising and revealing reversals. His plot, as theirs, flows precisely from the characters' attempts at plotting and counterplotting. Then his further develops a set of hesitant, merely temporary endings that reach a climax in the final scene of puzzling and surprising twists that seal his heroine's witty victory at every level. Such an interactive generation of rhetorical displays of wit, local plotting, and total emplotment, the "trappings" from microcosm to macrocosm, seemingly demonstrates the importance of a formal rhetorical approach to understanding *All's Well That Ends Well*, a set of problem plays in their dramatic history, and likely many other texts. The approach deeply implicates as well themes of human interaction.

The *Troilus and Cressida* chapter returns to a more readily identifiable traditional sense of rhetoric as linguistic display by examining three stylistic modes of displaying and persuasively employing wit, each named after a dominant character. At least as importantly, it turns to the most basic of all rhetorical concerns, the appeals to an audience made by way of logos, pathos, and ethos. Moreover, it especially focuses on rhetoric's most fundamental appeal—to ethos. Of enormous rhetorical interest is the dependence of all three styles on the appreciation of audiences, a confirmation of the abiding principle of reciprocal reflexivity between speaker and audience, as each is deeply responsive to and dependent on the other's perceived estimate of itself. While this ethical stylistic appeal is ostentatiously true of the wit of Pandarus (facile linguistic social interplay), it is equally true of the twofold wit of Ulysses (public proclamation of the self through pronouncements of received community values that prepare an audience to accept calculating analyses and proposals for action) and even of the wit of Thersites (scurrilous countering satiric commentaries). *Troilus and Cressida* blatantly presents egoistic displays of wit and drives for achievement as it anatomizes the rhetorical means of display of the self and of manipulation of others. Thus it presents what are likely central issues for all the Elizabethan-Jacobean problem plays—and what is likely the primary source of the fascinated consternation they rouse in critics.

Beyond displaying the three dominant styles as employed by other speakers, the Trojan council specifically displays how rhetorical appeals by way of pathos and especially of ethos prove far more persuasive than that by way of logos precisely because of the principle of reflexivity, the concern for the presentation of one's self as one imagines and desires that others perceive one. In the final section of the *Troilus and Cressida* essay, rhetorical and thematic approaches converge, and the usefulness of formal rhetorical analysis appears most obviously. Thus it represents an attempt to illustrate the usefulness to thematic interpretations of the formal considerations involved with audience response to and influence on a speaker. In examining the speaker's dependence on assumed common beliefs and his employment of these to affect the audience—and their reciprocal effect on him—it explores the thematics of ethos, shared beliefs, and persuasion. And it concludes that at the heart of this play resides a mutually reinforcing egoistic display and appreciation of manhood based on reputation for martial (and to a lesser degree sexual) exploit.

At first glance, the approach I am advocating might seem to turn back to formalism in ways I would regret and away from important theoretical, perspectival, methodological, and pedagogical contributions I want to hold on to. But I am offering merely a modest proposal for reformation that takes more account of formal analysis than is now common. My goals are to estimate the effectiveness of presentation, to test the persuasiveness of popular critical and historical interpretations of plays, specifically the problem plays, and to generate more interpretations of them still. The nexus that seems particularly useful between formal and other concerns is rhetorical study because of its advantageously expansive disciplinary interests. Since rhetoric intersects other disciplines in all kinds of ways, it offers a mode of mediation among issues in interpretation. Its major advantage over many other formalisms is that it undoes a false sense of objectivity that can ignore, or worse, implicitly oppose by excluding, a broad range of contexts. For poststructural, feminist and gender, material, postcolonial, new historical, cultural, and other studies emphasize and bring to the interpretation of texts a host of issues from academic fields ranging from philosophy, hermeneutics, and linguistics through the humanities and social sciences. Rhetoric's gauge of success is the effectiveness of forms and techniques for persuading audiences, based on the contingent presuppositions in interactions between speakers and auditors. Thus this formalism requires from the onset and in constant interaction attentiveness to the situation and the potential objectives of the text as these have been interpreted by critics trying to explain the fullest imaginable context of a text. While such a statement may hold true of necessity for other formalisms, the advantage rhetoric holds is not only that it rests on a long tradition of formal concerns, but that it has self-consciously examined these amidst the huge array of all the other concerns that have been considered or can conceivably be considered significant in specific situations.

My dual goal of testing current interpretations and of generating further ones explains why all of these essays reading rhetorically have depended more heavily than may be apparent on various interpretations. It obviously accounts for the early part of the introductory chapter, offering a historical sketch of the contours of rhetorical study in the early modern period so as to establish a credible claim for the pervasive, even dominant knowledge and employment of rhetoric by speakers and audiences, writers and readers in Renaissance England. This includes as well the establishment of the traditional principal divisions of rhetoric with emphasis on the appeals, invention, and ornamentation central throughout the study. It accounts less obviously but equally for the introduction's extension of this sketch into current rhetorical studies that expand on and sophisticate earlier rhetorical studies, since these accommodate further contributions that deepen our understanding of traditional rhetorical principles and practices. For to isolate ourselves from these is to sever ourselves from our own history and thus from self-conscious understanding of Renaissance English or any other history.

My dual goal of testing and generating interpretations also accounts for what likely seems an unlikely story of Harbage's abiding contribution to the study of the problem plays that dominated the era of Elizabeth's waning and James's waxing. It accounts all the more for the history of the transformations of Harbage's characterization of the problem plays in the two-thirds of a century since he formulated his hypothesis. By way of this recounting I am trying to establish the dual historical context within which I perceive the forms I concentrate on. In my view our perceptions of relevant late Elizabethan–early Jacobean history and literary history are inseparable from our reinvention or rediscovery of this history through our historical and critical attention to the problem plays. My interpretation deeply depends on constant self-conscious attention to this historical-critical complex because it provides the rhetorical hedge against formalism's tendencies toward the tediously detailed and arid, the irrelevant and inhumane, and the false implicature of objectivity. Thus, for example, I am especially interested in the increasing attention to the peripheries of the problem plays that Harbage castigated. Looking at those margins from different perspectives, agendas, and disciplines tells us about the foundations that the new history retained as it reacted against Harbage's assessment. For these different foci created our major shift in attention to the cosmopolitan and the commercial, the interactions and the hybridizations, that give us a very different sense of the incipient nationhood and national identity than Harbage assumed and proclaimed—but it does so on the grounds he laid out.

My characterization of the problem plays by their shared stylistic traits—the constituents of their tone—resumes my focus on formal considerations, but with history embedded in these examinations. For these provide the local forms that determine and enable the more historical and thematic concerns I find when I trace their employment through *Measure for Measure*, *All's Well That Ends Well*, and *Troilus and Cressida*. The introduction and first chapter, then, present most obviously my attempts to recount the essential historical understandings embedded in my foregrounded analyses of the formal techniques that make diverging historical recountings, critical interpretations possible.

Basically I am recommending an interactive formalism and contextualism that looks at how the themes are embedded in the formal patterns, since forms produce the coherence and cohesiveness that enable logical or at least consistent explanations. The multivalence, complement, disruption, and contrariness come more generally from the host of traditional and revisionist generalizations and their applications of different perspectives to the multitudinous specific historical references that different readers have found embedded in the formal patterns. The formal focus then supplies a ground or a blueprint usable to examine multiple, primary and contingent, complementary and antithetical, ironic, or other proposed views of texts. At the same time such a formal focus can generate further questions concerning the possible potential effects of a text's dominant or pervasive forms.

This modest proposal for reform does not amount to any new discovery, invention, or intervention. It amounts to a recovery, a reinvention, a reformulation of a mode rather neglected of late. The advantage of this formal rhetorical approach to plays is obvious for several reasons. First, in drama there is an onstage audience in addition to one offstage. Characters speak to each other, react and interact in ways that offer evidence for estimating the effects of the forms, their potential goals, causes and effects, and consequences. Second, there is no narrator in the huge majority of plays; *Pericles, Prince of Tyre*'s Gower is extraordinary. Thus explicit direction of responses by a narrator apart from the characters does not become an issue (this is not to deny that the author might employ an explicit or implicit choric commentary). So readings of the play, as opposed to stagings, offer a less easily influenced evaluation of the contests and contestants presented, witness the enormous variation in interpretations presented by stagings. Third, there is a foundational tradition in rhetoric for examining formally and contextually precisely this condition of presentation. Rhetoric has since Aristotle maintained an (in)famous interest in arguing *in utramque partem*, for both sides of a question proposed for debate, that has long been considered more expansively as trying out all conceivable arguments.

The advantage of a formal rhetorical approach for describing the problem plays of the late Elizabethan and early Jacobean era is also obvious. Their common forms make for an extraordinarily propitious presentation of what recent historicist critics have perceived to be troubled issues in simultaneously troubled and opportune times. And, consequently, they have earned extraordinarily mixed, conflicting, multiple thematic and allegorical interpretations in later times. While much literature can also be said to have generated such responses, the problem plays' meddling with generic horizons of expectation, their dark and troubled tone, their presentation of difficult—even intractable—personal, sexual, economic, and sociopolitical issues intensify the response well beyond what we anticipate in most literature and literary analyses. Formal rhetorical analysis helps to sort out these issues with their specific presentations. Moreover, it can form the initial impulse for and the constant check on hypotheses far beyond the figurations, emplotments, styles, reflexivities, and themes on which I have focused. The most obvious example would be the complex characterology Joel Fineman describes in *Shakespeare's Perjured Eye: The Invention of Poetic Subjectivity in the Sonnets*, a study that begins in, then extends and intensifies, the traditional rhetorical issues of epideictic's *laus* and *vituperatio* along with the multiply paradoxical figure of combination *syneciosis*.

The advantage of a formal rhetorical approach for describing other literary forms, such as sonnets, then, seems promising. The approach would seem propitious for lyrics as for drama because of the same general evasion of many of a narrator's potential interventions. The approach seems especially promising for lyrics such as those by Herbert or Marvell that present initially pellucid surface forms and immediately obvious themes but that under closer scrutiny and inside multiple contexts become surprisingly complex both formally and thematically. Nor does the approach seem unlikely for narratives, just more difficult because of additional questions involving the narrator's roles. Novels such as *Tristram Shandy* and *Ulysses* could conceivably yield interesting explanations to such an approach because of their play with rhetorical and narrative forms and models. But my brief is for specific application to drama and so any persuasion depends on my treatment of Shakespeare's three problem plays among their kind.

Notes

Chapter 1. Dark Comedies, Rhetoric, Shakespeare's Problem Plays

1. Howard, "Shakespeare and Genre," esp. 304–9; Yachnin, "Shakespeare's Problem Plays and the Drama of His Time." In addition to these prominent studies, a fairly sizable company of scholars has taken parallel paths along this general route. It includes studies centered on inns of court productions, such as William G. Elton's account of *Troilus and Cressida*; studies of these plays as social, political, and religious fin de siècle, such as Eric S. Mallin's contextual analysis of *Troilus and Cressida*; studies of the wars of the theaters such as James P. Bednarz's; and studies of patriarchal power relations such as Leonard Tennenhouse's, which focuses on the disappearing and surveilling monarch plays. Many of these I cite specifically later.

2. See, for example, the collection of essays edited by Mark David Rasmussen, *Renaissance Literature and Its Formal Engagements*.

3. Platt, "Shakespeare and Rhetorical Culture." His list of references offers an introductory bibliography to the approach among Shakespeareans.

4. For this rhetorical development see the suggestive account by Joel Altman in preparation for his impressive application of the techniques to drama, *The Tudor Play of Mind*, 31–63.

5. My digest outline focuses commonplaces with interlinkings through a host of early modern European, especially English, rhetoricians. It is documented and demonstrated in some detail by Mack, 76–102. It is further buttressed by the account of earlier backgrounds in Thomas M. Conley's *Rhetoric in the European Tradition*; by the perspective of representations of and responses to rhetoricians' self-images across western Europe in Rebhorn's *The Emperor of Men's Minds*; and by the assessment of Father Walter J. Ong in *Ramus, Method, and the Decay of Dialogue* and *Ramus and Talon Inventory*.

6. Frank Whigham and *Ambition and Privilege: The Social Tropes of Elizabethan Courtesy Theory* constitute one example of a scholar and study with which I am not concerned here (See 76 n. 3). Whigham basically assumes the breadth and depth of the matrix of authors and works, borrowings, imitations, and copious variations of early modern English discourse that Mack demonstrates. Since that assumption enables Whigham's extensions into the rhetorical formation of subjects and societies, Mack's very contribution multiplies Whigham's persuasive force. Conversely,

Whigham's contribution makes Mack's the more important. So where Mack lays blame, I would lay on praise. Perhaps Rebhorn provides mediation.

7. For a celebration and description, see Herbert W. Simons's introduction to his collection of essays by representative hands, *The Rhetorical Turn: Invention and Persuasion in the Conduct of Inquiry*. It is not insignificant that Thomas M. Conley's popular detailed historical outline, *Rhetoric in the European Tradition*, appeared the same year. Perhaps the most ambitious exploration came in the collection of essays emanating from yet another conference, A. G. Gross and W. M. Keith's *Rhetorical Hermeneutics: Invention and Interpretation in the Age of Science*.

8. See particularly Richard H. Lanham's *The Motives of Eloquence* and Brian Vickers's *In Defence of Rhetoric*.

Chapter 2. Dominant English Comedy at the Turn of the Seventeenth Century

1. *Shakespeare and the Rival Traditions* represents the culmination of Harbage's studies of the morality of the Shakespearean stage for the era of World War II. See especially *As They Liked It: An Essay on Shakespeare and Morality* and *Shakespeare's Audience*.

2. See Neely, *Broken Nuptials in Shakespeare's Plays*, 58ff, 225–26.

3. Jean E. Howard's suggestive expansion in "Shakespeare and Genre," 304–9, remains based in sexual and gender issues.

4. Butler, "Appendix II," in *Theatre and Crisis 1632–1642*, 293–306.

5. Knutson has constricted the interest in this issue in two ways: First, she demonstrates that it is not likely that Marston had a hand in writing *Histriomastix* (75–102) and, less demonstrably, that the "little eyases" passage in *Hamlet* is apparently a later addition (103–26). Second, she restricts the "poetomachia" to arguments over aesthetics and not over the commerce of the play companies, which she hypothesizes worked cooperatively, like a guild. The latter does not affect Bednarz's major point.

6. With minimal revision of focus and a different selection of plays and of historical criticism for evidence, Dollimore could have substituted "Dark Comedy" for "Tragedy" in *Radical Tragedy* and illuminated the most popular genre on the late Elizabethan–early Jacobean stage. The fact that his "Emergence" begins with Marston's *Antonio* plays and Shakespeare's *Troilus and Cressida* is more telling than fortuitous. I might add that *Antonio and Mellida* without the revenge tragedy in its second part has been labeled a problem play, a satirical comedy, and a tragicomedy.

7. Consider the interest roused by Richard Helgerson's discussions of mapping in *Forms of Nationhood*. See, for example, the collection of essays edited by Andrew Gordon and Bernhard Klein, *Literature, Mapping and the Politics of Space in Early Modern Britain*.

8. I quote and cite the New Mermaid edition of John Marston, *The Malcontent*, ed. Bernard Harris; the Yale edition of Ben Jonson, *The Alchemist*, ed. Alvin B. Ker-

nan; the New Mermaid edition of Thomas Middleton, *A Chaste Maid in Cheapside*, ed. Alan Brissenden; the Regents Renaissance Drama edition of George Chapman, *The Widow's Tears*, ed. Ethel M. Smeak; and, for *The Fleer*, *A Critical Old Spelling Edition of The Works of Edward Sharpham*, ed. Christopher Gordon Petter: 183–344.

9. Edward B. Partridge, *The Broken Compass*, esp. 51–62.

Chapter 3. Chiasmus, Justice, and Mercy, *Measure for Measure*

1. The definition comes from George Puttenham's 1589 *The Arte of English Poesie*, ed. Gladys Doidge Willcock and Alice Walker, 208; the description of uses from Henry Peacham's 1593, corrected and much enlarged edition of *The Garden of Eloquence*; the illustrations from *Hamlet* 2.2.98–99, 33–34, *Love's Labour's Lost* 1.2.18–19 (the most frequently quoted example of chiasmus from Shakespeare), *Measure for Measure* 3.1.182–83, 293–94, 5.1.14–16, 2.4.112–14. Throughout, for Shakespeare, unless I specify a different text, I cite and quote *The Norton Shakespeare*.

2. I follow the familiar rhetorical tradition that uses "figure" as the general term including both "tropes" such as metaphor that use a word to mean something beyond its customary meaning and "schemes" such as chiasmus that arrange words in patterns that call attention to themselves. But contrary to one common complementary pairing, I do not agree that schemes are merely "figures of sound" whereas tropes are "figures of thought"; schemes also change meanings.

3. I have found that Fahnestock provides a most useful historical account, analysis, application, and sourcebook. Of particular help is her introductory chapter outlining developments in rhetoric, including illustrations using *antimetabole*.

4. Carpenter, "The Essential Schemes of Syntax," 168, and "Stylistic Redundancy and Function in Discourse," 66.

5. Besides Parker's chapter in *Shakespeare from the Margins* (20–55), see her genealogy of seminal essays coming forward from the late 1970s and early 1980s to recent offspring (280–81 n. 5).

6. Vickers, *Classical Rhetoric in English Poetry*, 153.

7. The witness of many examples in the commentaries gathered by Mark Eccles for his New Variorum edition of *Measure for Measure* can be supplemented by Richard P. Wheeler's introductory overview of criticism that focuses problems and presents a selection of essays since then for his *Critical Essays on Shakespeare's "Measure for Measure."*

8. For a good account of the origins of equity courts in the ecclesiastical court traditions of Christian charity, see Shuger, *Political Theologies in Shakespeare's England*, 82–93.

9. However students judge the argumentative consequences of many deeply troubling psychological, social, and political issues introduced by Marc Shell in *The End*

of Kingship: "Measure for Measure," Incest, and the Ideal of Universal Siblinghood, all are indebted to the learning and scholarship he brings to bear, particularly in the chapters "Taliation, Part One: Punishment and Ransom" and "Taliation, Part Two: Likeness and Identity."

10. So explains J. W. Lever in his revised, 2nd New Arden edition of *Measure for Measure*. Lever's annotations, no less than those of Eccles, prove invaluable.

11. Gless, *"Measure for Measure," the Law, and the Convent*; Wheeler, *Shakespeare's Development and the Problem Comedies*; Dollimore, "Transgression and Surveillance in *Measure for Measure*"; Leonard Tennenhouse, "Family Rites; City Comedy, Romance, and the Strategies of Patriarchalism," in *Power on Display: The Politics of Shakespeare's Genres*, by Tennenhouse, 146–86, esp. 154–59; Wilson, "Prince of Darkness." Wheeler's *Critical Essays* collects most of the influential articles from this era; these particularly include various historicisms; in this volume, see especially Katharine Eisaman Maus's "Sexual Secrecy in *Measure for Measure*," taken from her *Inwardness and Theater in the English Renaissance*, and also her judicious and illuminating survey of problems and promises in her introduction to *Measure for Measure* in *The Norton Shakespeare*, 2021–27.

12. See Shuger, esp. 9–38; such is implicit as well in Tennenhouse, 157–59.

13. See Shuger's discussion about the distinctions between the "godly prince and the pirate king," the first whose sacred duty is to intervene on behalf of righteousness, the second who commits a trespass against God and subject (62–71). Whereas she places the dichotomy between the Duke and Angelo, I think the formal presentation in the play creates doubts about the Duke's virtue.

14. Maus, *Inwardness and Theater*, 172–77.

Chapter 4. The Trappings of *All's Well That Ends Well*

1. There are potential confusions over which Lord Dumaine can know what information in this scene and over their consistency in character in various scenes; and there is clear confusion over which leaves at the end of 3.6, and whether or not two different lords, or captains, are needed for scenes back in France while two remain in Florence. But none of these seems to have any significant effect on my case. So I make no changes to *The Norton Shakespeare*. For a full account of the data, see Wells and Taylor, eds., *William Shakespeare: A Textual Companion*, 492–93; for a clear explanation and discussion, see the Applause First Folio edition of *All's Well That Ends Well*, ed. Neil Freeman, xlii-xliv, and the notes.

2. Thanks to Jim Paxson and Eric Partridge's *Origins: A Short Etymological Dictionary of Modern English*, under "trappings" and "drap.3," for these useful derivations.

3. For suggestive development of these critical issues, see concisely Katharine Eisaman Maus's introduction to *All's Well* in *The Norton Shakespeare*, and expansively

Sheldon P. Zitner's Harvester New Critical Introduction to Shakespeare, *All's Well That Ends Well.*

4. Doran, *Endeavors of Art: A Study of Form in Elizabethan Drama*, 251. Gorfain, "Riddles and Reconciliation: Formal Unity in *All's Well That Ends Well*." I seek to intensify scrutiny of the style of the play in the context of its contemporaries.

5. For a comprehensive demonstration of the ubiquity and potency of "Proverbial Wisdom" during the era, see Adam Fox, *Oral and Literate Culture in England 1500–1700*, 112–72.

6. See Stanley E. Fish's "Georgics of the Mind: The Experience of Bacon's *Essays*," in *Self-Consuming Artifacts: The Experience of Seventeenth-Century Literature*, 78–155, especially the founding principles (86–90) and analyses (92ff.).

7. Gary Saul Morson, "*Aphoristic Style*: The Rhetoric of the Aphorism," in *A Companion to Rhetoric and Rhetorical Criticism*, ed. Jost and Olmsted, 248–65.

8. Parker, *Shakespeare from the Margins*, 189–90, initiates a long discussion with expansive implications.

9. For entry, see Parker, 192–93.

10. A strong case despite obvious difficulties has been made on Bertram's behalf by Richard P. Wheeler, *Shakespeare's Development and the Problem Comedies: Turn and Counter-Turn*, 35–91.

11. While Gorfain rightly sees Bertram's statements as central, she understates their importance as a "test, which he erected without realizing it" (267), similar perhaps to the typical tests of women by men prevalent in drama of the period. Moreover, she sees that the test "constitutes a riddle . . . acts as an implied question" (268). I take Bertram here to be making a knowing and direct challenge to Helen akin to challenges in other problem plays, especially in the totality of *All's Well*, which amounts to one riddling aphoristic challenge after another.

12. See Hunter's note for the pun.

13. Hunter's collection of the comments of past annotators on "dilemma," his text, 3.6.71, is especially helpful about uncertainties over whether Paroles is bragging of assured success or worrying about multiple possibilities of failure.

14. For an excellent statement about the measure of Helen's achievement in this entrapment through the emblematic ring exchange, albeit from a harsher, psychoanalytic perspective, see Janet Adelman, *Suffocating Mothers: Fantasies of Maternal Origin in Shakespeare's Plays, "Hamlet" to "The Tempest,"* 82.

15. See particularly Ian Donaldson's "*All's Well That Ends Well*: Shakespeare's Play of Endings" for suggesting multiple ends and endings as goals as well as potential resolutions; Parker, 197–204, for the most intricate treatment of deferrals; and Gerard J. Gross's "The Conclusion to *All's Well That Ends Well* for the impact of the final scene. Maus concisely sums up problems and praises in her introduction, 2178.

16. The elaborations of this final scene's entrapment of Bertram have drawn

inordinate critical abuse, perhaps in part because we have mainly forgone as cruel and unusual punishment the shaming rituals from public church confessions to the charivaris of weak husbands, the pillorying of disturbers of the peace to the carting of whores. These were not infrequent even among Shakespeare's own plays about this time, witness the humiliations of Falstaff for designing adultery in *The Merry Wives of Windsor* or the shaming progress through the streets of Claudio and Juliet for premarital sex in *Measure for Measure*, not to mention the shaming of Angelo at the climax of that play. For entry to related historical events, see D. E. Underdown's "The Taming of the Scold: The Enforcement of Patriarchal Authority in Early Modern England" and Martin Ingram's "Ridings, Rough Music and Mocking Rhymes in Early Modern England." For the same point from a different perspective, and so with different testimony, see Adelman, *Suffocating Mothers*, 284 n. 15.

Chapter 5. The Wit of Reflexivity in Shakespeare's *Troilus and Cressida*

1. Because of my thesis about wit and placement of the play among Elizabethan-Jacobean problem plays, instead of following *The Norton Shakespeare*, which takes the later Folio as its primary text (see Wells and Taylor's justification, *Textual Companion*, 424–43), for *Troilus and Cressida* I quote and cite the New Cambridge edition, ed. Anthony B. Dawson. Like many other editions, this takes the earlier quarto as its copy text. To sum up one position, while all agree to the authority of both, the Oxford Norton edition declares that the Folio text relies "on a copy of the quarto annotated by reference to a *Troilus and Cressida* manuscript substantively different from the manuscript that lies behind the quarto"; it incorporates subsequent changes. Its introduction of the new prologue and a few other passages plus its excision of the epistle and several other passages "slightly reduce the satiric elements in the portrayal of Troilus, Cressida, and Pandarus, and, more important, downplay the central love affair and shift the focus to the Trojan War itself" (1833). Dawson, however, observes that "the differences between the texts we are considering are fairly negligible. Of the 500 or so substantive variants, recent editors have agreed on the preferred reading in a large majority of cases. . . . whether one chooses Q or F as copy-text, the resulting editions will, in general terms, be quite similar" (251–52). I find David Bevington's textual introduction to his Arden Shakespeare edition of *Troilus and Cressida* the most readable and judicious summation of the many persuasive arguments about this play's text (398–429).

2. For a discussion of *Sejanus*, see Douglas A. Brooks, *From Playhouse to Printing House: Drama and Authorship in Early Modern England*, 40–53. For a proposed progression in the promotion of published plays that culminates when "during the reign of James I, printed plays started to be *treated* as literature," see Paul J. Voss, "Printing Conventions and the Early Modern Play." And for discussion of speculations about

puzzling evidence in the letter, see Bevington, in *Troilus and Cressida*, rev. 3rd Arden Shakespeare edition, 1–3, 400–401.

3. Peter Alexander first proposed this hypothesis in "*Troilus and Cressida*, 1609." A minutely detailed description of the play alongside what we know about revels productions has been made by William R. Elton in *"Troilus and Cressida" and the Inns of Court Revels*. It concentrates on the texture of diction, jargon, topics, references, and cynical tone of sidelong political and social commentary that displays rhetorical manipulation.

4. See the summations of criticism until almost 1950 by Hillebrand and T. W. Baldwin in the New Variorum edition of Shakespeare, *Troilus and Cressida*, ed. Harold N. Hillebrand.

5. I make no pretense of covering all the useful discussions of the play, only of referring to exemplary ones that seem to sum up critical tendencies and to have wide influence. The fullest coverage of criticism since the New Variorum edition that I know of is Bevington's introduction to his Arden edition; his detailed notes list agreements on different points and positions.

6. Maguire, "Performing Anger."

7. Engle, *Shakespearean Pragmatism*, 150–51.

8. See the sophisticated discussion in "Emulous Factions and the Collapse of Chivalry," in Mallin, *Inscribing the Time*, 25–61.

9. Charnes, "'So Unsecret to Ourselves': Notorious Identity and the Material Subject in *Troilus and Cressida*," in *Notorious Identity*, 70–102, and "The Two Party System in *Troilus and Cressida*."

10. Freund, "'Ariachne's broken woof'"; the quotation appears on 21.

11. Since most of these are prolific publishers, I provide only entries to their works. For George Herbert Mead see especially *Philosophy of the Act*; for Erving Goffman, *The Presentation of Self in Everyday Life*; for Philip G. Zimbardo, *Influencing Attitudes and Changing Behavior*, with others; for Peter L. Berger and Thomas Luckmann, *The Social Construction of Reality*; for Pierre Bourdieu, *Outline of a Theory of Practice*; for Anthony Giddens, *The Constitution of Society: Outline of the Theory of Structuration*.

12. McAlindon, "Language, Style, and Meaning in *Troilus and Cressida*." We will return to parallels between McAlindon's first term and Parker's insightful discourse and materialist analysis of "dilation," the turgid or swollen style that forms the excess of the grand style described most popularly in the *Rhetorica ad Herennium* (Parker, *Shakespeare from the Margins*: 220–28).

13. I can make no attempt to supply a representative sampling of the enormous corpus of explanations, extensions, revisions, applications from the Bakhtin enterprise.

14. Danson, *Tragic Alphabet*, 68–96.

15. Gaonkar, "Introduction: Contingency and Probability," 8.

16. For quotation and brief analysis of parallels, see the appendix "Ulysses on 'Degree'" to the Variorum edition by Hillebrand and Baldwin, 389–410, specifically 390–91, 394–95. Ultimately the effect of this speech is open to considerable skepticism on several grounds described by David Norbrook in his learned and influential "Rhetoric, Ideology, and the Elizabethan World Picture." Norbrook is persuasive that the Renaissance rhetorical tradition was simultaneously more prone to consider analogy useful to gain immediate practical effect and as well to consider analogy more vulnerable to skeptical reception than earlier (142, 143, 147), that Renaissance considerations of Ulysses' brilliant rhetorical skills and speeches were widely admired for their effectiveness but equally widely suspect for his shifty shrewdness (144–45), and that Sir John Davies's *Orchestra*'s similar analogy was not merely open to critique but was in fact severely criticized by his contemporary rhetorician John Hoskyns (147–54). Then, in a fine analysis Norbrook argues that Ulysses' speech on degree "is involved in a series of somewhat devious rhetorical strategies to secure the unity of the Greek forces . . . and there is a gap between the lofty vision of natural harmony invoked by Ulysses and the speech act he is performing, of persuading the leaders to engage in a shabby tactical trick" (155ff). My perspective from the view of the conditions under which the speech is delivered in council and of its complicit onstage audience emphasizes the speech's great immediate effectiveness. Thus I do not hear the skeptical reaction during the first great evocation of degree that seems to gain wide assent in principle. Rather the skeptical reaction appears with the shift in tone that comes with the Machiavellian application.

17. For a representative digest and an approving tone, see Hillebrand and Baldwin's Variorum edition, 397–410, and then, for the more current skeptical context see Norbrook.

18. For the parallel patterns and significant diversions, see Kenneth Palmer's introduction to his 2nd Arden edition of *Troilus and Cressida*, 41–49.

19. Adamson, Twayne's New Critical Introductions to Shakespeare: *Troilus and Cressida*, 43–44.

20. For an array of terms see Hillebrand's Variorum edition, 562–68, and Bevington's 3rd Arden Shakespeare edition, 79–84, with the references in his notes.

21. Colie, *Shakespeare's Living Art*, 317–49. For extensions see Bevington, rev. 3rd Arden Shakespeare edition, 80–83.

22. See Bruce Boehrer, "The Matter of Troy," 72–75, in "The Privy and Its Double," in *A Companion to Shakespeare Studies*, ed. Dutton and Howard, 4.

23. See, for example, Burke, *A Rhetoric of Motives*, 55–59ff.

Works Cited

Adamson, Jane. Twayne's New Critical Introductions to Shakespeare: *Troilus and Cressida*. Boston: Twayne, 1987.

Adelman, Janet. *Suffocating Mothers: Fantasies of Maternal Origin in Shakespeare's Plays, "Hamlet" to "The Tempest."* London: Routledge, 1992.

Alexander, Peter. "*Troilus and Cressida*, 1609." *Library* 9 (1929): 267–86.

Altman, Joel. *The Tudor Play of Mind*. Berkeley and Los Angeles: University of California Press, 1978.

Anderson, Benedict. *Imagined Communities: Reflections on the Origin and Spread of Nationalism*. Rev. ed. London: Verso, 1991.

Auerbach, Erich. *Mimesis: The Representation of Reality in Western Literature*. Princeton, N.J.: Princeton University Press, 1953.

Bednarz, James P. *Shakespeare and the Poets' War*. New York: Columbia University Press, 2001.

Berger, Peter L., and Thomas Luckmann. *The Social Construction of Reality*. Garden City, N.Y.: Doubleday, 1966.

Boas, F. S. *Shakespeare and His Predecessors*. New York: Charles Scribner's Sons, 1896.

Bourdieu, Pierre. *Outline of a Theory of Practice*. Translated by Richard Nice. Cambridge, England: Cambridge University Press, 1977.

Bowen, Barbara E. *Gender in the Theater of War: Shakespeare's "Troilus and Cressida."* New York: Garland, 1993.

Brooks, Douglas A. *From Playhouse to Printing House: Drama and Authorship in Early Modern England*. New York: Cambridge University Press, 2000.

Bruster, Douglas. *Drama and the Market in the Age of Shakespeare*. Cambridge, England: Cambridge University Press, 1992.

Burke, Kenneth. *A Rhetoric of Motives*. New York: Prentice-Hall, 1950.

Butler, Martin. *Theatre and Crisis 1632–1642*. Cambridge, England: Cambridge University Press, 1984.

Campbell, Oscar James. *Comicall Satyre and Shakespeare's "Troilus and Cressida."* San Marino, Calif.: Huntington Library, 1938.

Carpenter, Ronald H. "The Essential Schemes of Syntax: An Analysis of Rhetorical Theory's Recommendations for Uncommon Word Orders." *Quarterly Journal of Speech* 55 (1969): 161–68.

———. "Stylistic Redundancy and Function in Discourse." *Language and Style* 3 (1970): 62–68.

Chapman, George. *The Widow's Tears*. Edited by Ethel M. Smeak. Regents Renaissance Drama edition. Lincoln: University of Nebraska Press, 1966.

Charnes, Linda. *Notorious Identity: Materializing the Subject in Shakespeare*. Cambridge, Mass.: Harvard University Press, 1993.

———. "The Two Party System in *Troilus and Cressida*." In *A Companion to Shakespeare Studies,* edited by Richard Dutton and Jean E. Howard, 4: 302–15. Oxford, England: Blackwell, 2003.

Clark, Ira. *Comedy, Youth, Manhood in Early Modern England*. Newark: University of Delaware Press, 2003.

———. "Measure for Measure: Chiasmus, Justice, and Mercy." *Style* 35 (Winter 2001): 659–80.

———. *The Moral Art of Philip Massinger*. Lewisburg, Pa.: Bucknell University Press, 1993.

———. *Professional Playwrights: Massinger, Ford, Shirley, and Brome*. Lexington: University Press of Kentucky, 1992.

———. "The Trappings of *All's Well That Ends Well*." *Style* 39 (Fall 2005): 277–98.

Colie, Rosalie L. *Shakespeare's Living Art*. Princeton, N.J.: Princeton University Press, 1974.

Conley, Thomas M. *Rhetoric in the European Tradition*. White Plains, N.Y.: Longman, 1990.

Cook, Ann Jennalie. *The Privileged Playgoers of Shakespeare's London*. Princeton, N.J.: Princeton University Press, 1981.

Curtius, Ernst Robert. *European Literature and the Latin Middle Ages*. Translated by Willard R. Trask. New York: Harper and Row, 1953.

Danson, Lawrence. *Tragic Alphabet: Shakespeare's Drama of Language*. New Haven, Conn.: Yale University Press, 1974.

Dillon, Janette. *Theatre, Court and City, 1595–1610*. Cambridge, England: Cambridge University Press, 2000.

Dollimore, Jonathan. *Radical Tragedy: Religion, Ideology and Power in the Drama of Shakespeare and His Contemporaries*. Brighton, England: Harvester Press; Chicago: University of Chicago Press, 1984.

———. "Transgression and Surveillance in *Measure for Measure.*" In *Political Shakespeare*, edited by Jonathan Dollimore and Alan Sinfield, 72–87. Manchester, England: Manchester University Press, 1985.

Donaldson, Ian. "*All's Well That Ends Well*: Shakespeare's Play of Endings." *Essays in Criticism* 27 (1977): 34–55.

Doran, Madeleine. *Endeavors of Art: A Study of Form in Elizabethan Drama*. Madison: University of Wisconsin Press, 1954.

———. *Shakespeare's Dramatic Language*. Madison: University of Wisconsin Press, 1976.

Dutton, Richard, and Jean E. Howard, eds. *A Companion to Shakespeare Studies*. Oxford, England: Blackwell, 2003.

Elam, Keir. *Shakespeare's Universe of Discourse: Language-Games in the Comedies*. Cambridge, England: Cambridge University Press, 1984.

Elton, William R. *"Troilus and Cressida" and the Inns of Court Revels*. Aldershott, England: Ashgate, 2000.

Empson, William. "Sense in *Measure for Measure*." In *The Structure of Complex Words*, 270–88. London: New Directions, 1951.

Engle, Lars. *Shakespearean Pragmatism: Market of His Time*. Chicago: University of Chicago Press, 1993.

Fahnestock, Jeanne. *Rhetorical Figures in Science*. New York: Oxford University Press, 1999.

Fineman, Joel. *Shakespeare's Perjured Eye: The Invention of Poetic Subjectivity in the Sonnets*. Berkeley and Los Angeles: University of California Press, 1986.

Finkelpearl, Philip J. *John Marston of the Middle Temple: An Elizabethan Dramatist in His Social Setting*. Cambridge, Mass.: Harvard University Press, 1969.

Fish, Stanley E. *Self-Consuming Artifacts: The Experience of Seventeenth-Century Literature*. Berkeley and Los Angeles University of California Press, 1972.

Fox, Adam. *Oral and Literate Culture in England 1500–1700*. Oxford, England: Clarendon Press, 2000.

Freund, Elizabeth. "'Ariachne's broken woof': The Rhetoric of Citation in *Troilus and Cressida*." In *Shakespeare and the Question of Theory*, edited by Patricia Parker and Geoffrey Hartman, 19–36. New York: Methuen, 1985.

Gaonkar, Dilip Parmeshwar. "Introduction: Contingency and Probability." In *A Companion to Rhetoric and Rhetorical Criticism*, edited by Walter Jost and Wendy Olmsted, 5–21. Oxford, England: Blackwell, 2004.

Genette, Gerard. *Narrative Discourse: An Essay in Method*. Translated by Jane E. Lewin. Ithaca, N.Y.: Cornell University Press, 1980.

Gerard, René. "The Politics of Desire in *Troilus and Cressida*." In *Shakespeare and the Question of Theory*, edited by Patricia Parker and Geoffrey Hartman, 188–209. New York: Methuen, 1985.

Gibbons, Brian. *Jacobean City Comedy: A Study of Satiric Plays by Jonson, Marston, and Middleton*. Cambridge, Mass.: Harvard University Press, 1968.

Giddens, Anthony. *The Constitution of Society: Outline of the Theory of Structuration*. Berkeley and Los Angeles: University of California Press, 1984.

Gless, Darryl. *"Measure for Measure," the Law, and the Convent*. Princeton, N.J.: Princeton University Press, 1979.

Goffman, Erving. *The Presentation of Self in Everyday Life*. Garden City, N.Y.: Doubleday, 1959.

Gordon, Andrew, and Bernhard Klein, eds. *Literature, Mapping and the Politics of Space in Early Modern Britain*. Cambridge, England: Cambridge University Press, 2001.

Gorfain, Phyllis. "Riddles and Reconciliation: Formal Unity in *All's Well That Ends Well*." *Journal of the Folklore Institute* 13 (1976): 263–81.

Gross, A. G., and W. M. Keith, eds. *Rhetorical Hermeneutics: Invention and Interpretation in the Age of Science*. Albany: State University of New York Press, 1997.

Gross, Gerard J. "The Conclusion to *All's Well That Ends Well*." *Studies in English Literature 1500–1900* 23 (1983): 157–75.

Group [Mu], J. Dubois, et al. *A General Rhetoric*. Translated by Paul B. Burrell and Edgar M. Slotkin. Baltimore: Johns Hopkins University Press, 1981.

Gurr, Andrew. *Playgoing in Shakespeare's London*. Cambridge, England: Cambridge University Press, 1987.

———. *The Shakespearian Playing Companies*. Oxford, England: Clarendon Press, 1996.

Harbage, Alfred. *As They Liked It: An Essay on Shakespeare and Morality*. New York: Macmillan, 1947.

———. *Shakespeare and the Rival Traditions*. New York: Macmillan, 1952.

———. *Shakespeare's Audience*. New York: Columbia University Press, 1941.

Hawkins, Harriett. Twayne's New Critical Introductions to Shakespeare: *Measure for Measure*. Boston: Twayne, 1987.

Haydn, Hiram. *The Counter-Renaissance*. New York: Charles Scribner's Sons, 1950.

Helgerson, Richard. *Forms of Nationhood: The Elizabethan Writing of England*. Chicago: University of Chicago Press, 1992.

Howard, Jean E. "Mastering Difference in *The Dutch Courtesan*." *Shakespeare Studies* 24 (1996): 105–17.

———. "Shakespeare and Genre." In *A Companion to Shakespeare*, edited by David Scott Kastan, 297–310. Oxford, England: Blackwell, 1999.

———. "Women, Foreigners, and the Regulation of Urban Space in *Westward Ho*." In *Historical London, ca. 1600*, edited by Lena Cowen Orlin, 150–67. Philadelphia: University of Pennsylvania Press, 2000.

Hunter, G. K. *English Drama 1586–1642: The Age of Shakespeare*. Oxford, England: Clarendon Press, 1997.

———. "English Folly and Italian Vice: The Moral Landscape of John Marston." In *Jacobean Theatre*, edited by John Russell Brown, 84–111. Stratford-upon-Avon Studies 1. New York: St. Martin's Press, 1960.

Ingram, Martin. "Ridings, Rough Music and Mocking Rhymes in Early Modern

England." In *Popular Culture in Seventeenth-Century England*, edited by Barry Reay, 166–97. New York: St. Martin's Press, 1985.

Jonson, Ben. *The Alchemist*. Edited by Alvin B. Kernan. New Haven, Conn.: Yale University Press, 1974.

Joseph, Sister Miriam. *Shakespeare's Use of the Arts of Language*. New York: Columbia University Press, 1946.

Jost, Walter, and Wendy Olmsted, eds. *A Companion to Rhetoric and Rhetorical Criticism*. Oxford, England: Blackwell, 2004.

Kernan, Alvin. *The Cankered Muse: Satire of the English Renaissance*. New Haven, Conn.: Yale University Press, 1959.

Knight, G. Wilson. *The Wheel of Fire: Interpretations of Shakespearian Tragedy*. London: Methuen, 1949.

Knights, L. C. *Drama and Society in the Age of Jonson*. London: Chatto and Windus, 1937.

Knutson, Roslyn Lander. *Playing Companies and Commerce in Shakespeare's Time*. Cambridge, England: Cambridge University Press, 2001.

Lanham, Richard H. *The Motives of Eloquence: Literary Rhetoric in the Renaissance*. New Haven, Conn.: Yale University Press, 1976.

Lawrence, W. W. *Shakespeare's Problem Comedies*. New York: Columbia University Press, 1931.

Leggatt, Alexander. *Citizen Comedy in the Age of Shakespeare*. Toronto: University of Toronto Press, 1973.

Leinwand, Theodore B. *The City Staged: Jacobean Comedy, 1603–1613*. Madison: University of Wisconsin Press, 1986.

Mack, Peter. *Elizabethan Rhetoric: Theory and Practice*. Cambridge, England: Cambridge University Press, 2002.

Maguire, Laurie E. "Performing Anger: The Anatomy of Abuse(s) in *Troilus and Cressida*." *Renaissance Drama* 31 (2002): 153–83.

Mahood, M. M. *Shakespeare's Wordplay*. London: Methuen, 1957.

Mallin, Eric S. *Inscribing the Time: Shakespeare and the End of Elizabethan England*. Berkeley and Los Angeles: University of California Press, 1995.

Marston, John. *Antonio and Mellida*. Edited by G. K. Hunter. Regents Renaissance Drama edition. Lincoln: University of Nebraska Press, 1965.

———. *The Malcontent*. Edited by Bernard Harris. New Mermaid edition. London: Ernest Benn, 1967.

———. *The Malcontent*. Edited by G. K. Hunter. Revels Plays edition. London: Methuen, 1975.

Maus, Katharine Eisaman. *Inwardness and Theater in the English Renaissance*. Chicago: University of Chicago Press, 1995.

McAlindon, T. "Language, Style, and Meaning in *Troilus and Cressida*." *PMLA* 84 (1969): 29–43.

Mead, George Herbert. *Philosophy of the Act*. Chicago: University of Chicago Press, 1938.

Middleton, Thomas. *A Chaste Maid in Cheapside*. Edited by Alan Brissenden. New Mermaid edition. 2nd impression. London: Ernest Benn, 1974.

Nanny, Max. "Chiasmus in Literature: Ornament or Function?" *Word and Image* 4 (1988): 51–59.

Neely, Carol Thomas. *Broken Nuptials in Shakespeare's Plays*. New Haven, Conn.: Yale University Press, 1985.

Norbrook, David. "Rhetoric, Ideology, and the Elizabethan World Picture." In *Renaissance Rhetoric*, edited by Peter Mack, 140–64. London: St. Martin's, 1994.

Ong, Walter J. *Ramus and Talon Inventory*. Cambridge, Mass.: Harvard University Press, 1958.

———. *Ramus, Method, and the Decay of Dialogue.* Cambridge, Mass.: Harvard University Press, 1958.

Parker, Patricia. *Shakespeare from the Margins: Language, Culture, Context*. Chicago: University of Chicago Press, 1996.

Partridge, Edward B. *The Broken Compass: A Study of the Major Comedies of Ben Jonson*. London: Chatto and Windus, 1964.

Partridge, Eric. *Origins: A Short Etymological Dictionary of Modern English*. London: Routledge and Kegan Paul, 1966.

Paster, Gail Kern. *The Idea of the City in the Age of Shakespeare*. Athens: University of Georgia Press, 1985.

Peacham, Henry. *The Garden of Eloquence*. STC 19498, in *A Short-Title Catalogue of Books Printed in England, Scotland, and Ireland and of English Books Printed Abroad, 1475–1640*. London: Bibliographical Society, 1593.

Perelman, Ch., and L. Olbrechts-Tyteca. *The New Rhetoric: A Treatise on Argumentation*. Translated by John Wilkinson and Purcell Weaver. Notre Dame, Ind.: University of Notre Dame Press, 1969.

Platt, Peter G. "Shakespeare and Rhetorical Culture." In *A Companion to Shakespeare*, edited by David Scott Kastan, 276–96. Oxford, England: Blackwell, 1999.

Puttenham, George. *The Arte of English Poesie*. Edited by Gladys Doidge Willcock and Alice Walker. Cambridge, England: Cambridge University Press, 1936.

Quilligan, Maureen. *The Language of Allegory: Defining the Genre*. Ithaca, N.Y.: Cornell University Press, 1979.

Rasmussen, Mark David. *Renaissance Literature and Its Formal Engagements*. New York: Palgrave, 2002.

Rebhorn, Wayne A. *The Emperor of Men's Minds: Literature and the Renaissance Discourse of Rhetoric*. Ithaca, N.Y.: Cornell University Press, 1995.

Shakespeare, William. *All's Well That Ends Well*. Edited by G. K. Hunter. Arden edition. London: Methuen, 1957.

———. *All's Well That Ends Well*. Edited by Neil Freeman. New York: Applause Theatre Books, 2001.

———. *Measure for Measure*. Edited by J. W. Lever. Rev. 2nd New Arden Shakespeare edition. London: Methuen, 1965.

———. *Measure for Measure*. Edited by Mark Eccles. New Variorum edition. New York: Modern Language Association of America, 1980.

———. *The Norton Shakespeare*. Based on the Oxford edition. Edited by Stephen Greenblatt, Walter Cohen, Jean E. Howard, and Katharine Eisaman Maus. New York: Norton, 1997.

———. *Troilus and Cressida*. Edited by Harold N. Hillebrand. New Variorum edition. Philadelphia: Lippincott, 1953.

———. *Troilus and Cressida*. Edited by Kenneth Palmer. Rev. 2nd Arden Shakespeare edition. London: Methuen, 1982.

———. *Troilus and Cressida*. Edited by David Bevington. Rev. 3rd Arden Shakespeare edition. Walton-on-Thames, England: Thomas Nelson, 1998.

———. *Troilus and Cressida*. Edited by Anthony B. Dawson. New Cambridge edition. Cambridge, England: Cambridge University Press, 2003.

Shapiro, Michael. *Children of the Revels: The Boy Companies of Shakespeare's Time and Their Plays*. New York: Columbia University Press, 1977.

Sharpham, Edward. *A Critical Old Spelling Edition of The Works of Edward Sharpham*. Edited by Christopher Gordon Petter. Vol. 18 of *The Renaissance Imagination*. New York: Garland, 1986.

Shell, Marc. *The End of Kingship: "Measure for Measure," Incest, and the Ideal of Universal Siblinghood*. Stanford, Calif.: Stanford University Press, 1988.

Shuger, Debora Kuller. *Political Theologies in Shakespeare's England: The Sacred and the State in "Measure for Measure."* Houndmills, England: Palgrave, 2001.

Simons, Herbert W., ed. *The Rhetorical Turn: Invention and Persuasion in the Conduct of Inquiry*. Chicago: University of Chicago Press, 1990.

Sloane, Thomas O., editor in chief. *Encyclopedia of Rhetoric*. New York: Oxford University Press, 2001.

Smith, Emma. "'So much English by the Mother': Gender, Foreigners, and the Mother Tongue in William Haughton's *Englishmen for My Money*." *Medieval and Renaissance Drama in England* 13 (2001): 165–81.

Tennenhouse, Leonard. *Power on Display: The Politics of Shakespeare's Genres*. London: Methuen, 1986.

Underdown, D. E. "The Taming of the Scold: The Enforcement of Patriarchal Authority in Early Modern England." In *Order and Disorder in Early Modern England*, edited by Anthony Fletcher and John Stevenson, 116–36. Cambridge, England: Cambridge University Press, 1985.

Vickers, Brian. *Classical Rhetoric in English Poetry*. London: Macmillan, 1970.

———. *In Defence of Rhetoric*. Oxford, England: Clarendon Press, 1988.

Voss, Paul J. "Printing Conventions and the Early Modern Play." *Medieval and Renaissance Drama in England* 15 (2003): 98–115.

Wells, Stanley E., and Gary Taylor, eds. *William Shakespeare: A Textual Companion*. Oxford, England: Clarendon Press, 1987.

Wheeler, Richard P. *Critical Essays on Shakespeare's "Measure for Measure."* New York: G. K. Hall, 1999.

———. *Shakespeare's Development and the Problem Comedies: Turn and Counter-Turn*. Berkeley and Los Angeles: University of California Press, 1981.

Whigham, Frank. *Ambition and Privilege: The Social Tropes of Elizabethan Courtesy Theory*. Berkeley and Los Angeles: University of California Press, 1984.

Wilson, Richard. "Prince of Darkness: Foucault's Shakespeare." In *"Measure for Measure": Theory in Practice*, edited by Nigel Wood, 133–78. Buckingham, England: Open University Press, 1996.

Yachnin, Paul. "Shakespeare's Problem Plays and the Drama of His Time: *Troilus and Cressida, All's Well That Ends Well, Measure for Measure*." In *A Companion to Shakespeare's Works*, edited by Richard Dutton and Jean E. Howard, 4: 46–68. Oxford, England: Blackwell, 2003.

Zimbardo, Philip G. *Influencing Attitudes and Changing Behavior*. Reading, Mass.: Addison-Wesley, 1977.

Zitner, Sheldon P. *All's Well That Ends Well*. New York: Harvester Wheatsheaf, 1989.

Index

Ira Clark is professor of English at the University of Florida. He has published numerous essays and reviews on a wide variety of topics in early modern English poetry and drama and is author of *Christ Revealed: The History of the Neotypological Lyric in the English Renaissance*; *Professional Playwrights: Massinger, Ford, Shirley, and Brome*; *The Moral Art of Philip Massinger*; and *Comedy, Youth, Manhood in Early Modern England*.